W9-DDG-863

BY THE AUTO EDITORS OF CONSUMER GUIDE®

MUSCLE CARS OF THE '50s

PUBLICATIONS
INTERNATIONAL, LTD.

CONTENTS

Copyright © 1992 by Publications International, Ltd. All rights reserved. This book may not be reproduced or quoted in whole or in part by mimeograph or any other printed or electronic means, or for presentation on radio, television, videotape, or film without written permission from:

Louis Weber, C.E.O.
Publications International, Ltd.
7373 North Cicero Avenue
Lincolnwood, Illinois 60646

Permission is never granted for commercial purposes.

Printed and bound in U.S.A.

8 7 6 5 4 3 2 1

ISBN: 1-56173-301-6

CREDITS

Owners
Special thanks to the owners of the cars featured in this book for their enthusiastic cooperation. They are listed below along with the page numbers(s) on which their cars appear:

John M. Galandak 6; **Gary L. Walker** 7; **Russ & Shirley Dawson** 8; **Mary Jaeger** 8; **Tom & Karen Barnes** 9; **Phillip Kuhn** 12, 13; **Frank R. Bobek** 18, 19; **Jerry Hammer** 19; **Marie Martin & Bob Wahers** 19; **Jim Van Gondon** 20; **Jim Cahill** 21; **Paul Eggerling** 21; **Gary Johns** 22; **Eugine R. Siuda, Jr.** 23; **Bill Bodnarchuck** 24; **Bill Goodsene** 25; **Gary Mills** 26, 27; **Stephen Capone** 27, 28; **Edward S. Kuziel** 29; **Jeff Dranson** 30; **Pete Bogard** 31, 32; **Robert & Diane Adams** 33; **Otto T. Rosenbusch** 36, 37; **George Berg** 41; **Richard Carpenter** 41; **Roger & Connie Graeber** 42-43, 44; **Don Armstrong** 45; **Gaylen & Fay Erb** 46, 47; **Bob Shapiro** 49; **Bill Hill** 50; **Marvin**

& Joan Hughes 51; Neil Vedder 52; Tom Franks 53; Jim Goldheimer 53; Ray & Nancy Deitke 54; David M. Leslie 54; Donald Kish, Sr. 55; Dr. Ollie P. Williams 57, 58; Doug Burnell 59, 60; Rod Morris, Classic Cars, Jacksonville, FL 62, 63; Roger Clements 63; H.H. Wheeler, Jr. 63; Ross Gibaldi 65, 66; R.G. Brelsford 67; Phillip Arneson 68; Bud Juneau 69; Bill Wagaman 69; Fraser Dante LTD, Roswell, GA 70, 71; Greg Munro 72, 73, 74; Duane & Steven Stupienski 73; M.J. Strumpf 75; Ray & Marilyn Benot 76-77; Bob Peiler 76, 77; Thomas L. Karkiewicz 78; Paul Oxley 80; Lloyd Groshond 81; Richard Carpenter 82; Ken Regnier 85, 87; Dennis M. Statz 86; Glenn R. Bappe 88, 89; Dr. William H. Lenharth 91, 92; Roger Fonk 92; Ken Perry 93; Bob Patrick 94, 95.

Photography
The editors would like to thank the following people and organizations for supplying the photography that made this book possible. They are listed below, along with the page number(s) of their photos:

Philip Arneson 68; Scott Baxter 7; Michael Brown 63; Mitch Frumkin 8; Thomas Glatch 86; Sam Griffith 21, 24, 31, 32; Jerry Heasley 58; Fergus Hernandes 20; Bill Hill 50; Bud Juneau 26, 27, 42-43, 44, 59, 60, 61, 67, 69, 93, 94, 95; Tim Kerwin 91, 92; Milton Gene Kieft 53, 54, 55, 65, 66; Dan Lyons 27, 28; Vince Manocchi 19, 33, 38, 39, 41, 61, 63, 64, 82; Doug Mitchel 18, 19, 22, 23, 40, 41, 46, 47, 57, 58, 69, 76-77, 81, 85, 87, 88, 89, 92; Mike Mueller 6, 8, 23, 29, 51, 62, 63; Jay Peck 70, 71; Frank Peiler 57; Phillips Camera House 52; Greg Price 73; Richard Spiegelman 11, 44, 46; Marvin Terrell 49; Nicky Wright 9, 25, 36, 37, 53, 54, 72, 73, 74, 78, 79.

Very special thanks to: Karl St. Antoine, Chevrolet PR; Chrysler Historical Collection; Helen J. Earley, Oldsmobile History Center; Larry Gustin, Buick Motor PR; Ford Photographic; Pontiac PR.

Introduction: The Dawn of the Muscle-Car Age

Most everybody knows that the "muscle car" era extended from 1964, when Pontiac's first hot GTO appeared on the scene, to the early Seventies, when rising insurance rates and more restrictive government emissions rules brought down the curtain on one of the most exciting eras in American automotive history.

How, then, a book on *Muscle Cars of the '50s*? Actually, there are a number of good reasons, one being that the "muscle car" has always been with us. Consider, for example, the earliest Fords, which with old Henry's penchant for light weight were among the quickest on the road. And reasonably affordable, too! Or how about the early

Teens' Stutz Bearcat? At $2000—the price of a decent house—not too many people could afford one, but the legend of spoiled college brats racing around in those rakish roadsters lives on even now. Despite the Great Depression, performance was never more affordable than in 1932, the year Henry Ford unleashed his hot new flathead V-8. For as little as $460, one could easily embarrass the likes of a Classic Pack-

ard, or most any other car made in America, or elsewhere for that matter.

World War II, perhaps the most disruptive event in human history, put a damper on many things. But America rose to the occasion, and when the killing was finally over, people looked forward to a better tomorrow. Among their priorities were better housing, better education, a better life in general—and that included new cars. At first it didn't matter what kind of car, or how it was equipped, because a car-starved public stood in line to buy most anything on wheels. The automakers knew, however, that once demand was filled they would have to go back to the good old-fashioned business of selling cars, rather than just taking orders. And if anything good came out of the

war, it was a lot of new technology (metallurgy, in particular), some of it applicable to the engineering of improved automobiles.

Automakers spent the first few years just filling the pent-up demand, of course, but even while they were doing that their engineers and stylists were readying all-new cars. Insofar as performance was concerned, it's generally acknowledged that General Motors fired the first shot with its new 1949 Cadillac and Oldsmobile overhead-valve, short-stroke V-8s. Though they really weren't designed so much for power as smoothness, durability, and economy, performance was an enticing side benefit that the public couldn't overlook. And didn't.

Some auto historians will tell you that the "horsepower race" actually began in 1951, when Chrysler introduced its brilliant new hemispherical-head V-8, the legendary "Hemi." Likely, they're right, because with its 180 horsepower, the Hemi outpowered its GM rivals—which of course meant that they had to respond in kind. Indeed, the ohv V-8 was not only the key to performance in the Fifties, it was also the key to corporate survival. Consider, for example, the makes that never offered one. Hudson, despite its racing successes chronicled within these pages, didn't, and it became the minor partner in a "merger" with Nash in 1954 to form American Motors Corporation. AMC *did* develop a V-8, and

survived into 1987, when it was taken over by Chrysler Corporation. Kaiser-Frazer, despite way-ahead 1951 styling and some of the most beautiful interiors ever seen in any automobile, had a 288-cid V-8 under development, but never had the cash to bring it out. K-F was out of the American market by 1955. Willys never got around to a V-8 either, and was absorbed by Kaiser in 1953. Among the independents, Studebaker was the most astute when it came to forward-looking engineering: It had an ohv V-8 in 1951, not to mention a fully automatic transmission in late 1950. Its reward was that, unlike most independents, it survived as an automaker into the mid-Sixties. Packard, for nearly half a century America's premier luxury-car builder, finally replaced its tough and durable straight-eight engines with more powerful and lively V-8s for 1955, but had made the disastrous mistake of not only waiting too long, but of becoming allied with money-losing Studebaker in 1954.

But while some makes disappeared during the "Fabulous Fifties," others went from strength to strength. Often that related to the incredible performance gains made during that decade. Ford, originally the acknowledged performance leader in the low-price field, went from 100 horsepower in 1950 to a maximum of 300 in 1959—exactly triple! Plymouth went from 97 horses to 305. And Chevy, which started with a 90-horse "Stovebolt Six," ended the Fifties with an incredible 315 horses—double the output of the most powerful and expensive makes at the beginning of the decade.

The point here, of course, is that there *were* "muscle cars" in the Fifties, even though they weren't called that at the time, and that's what this book is all about. It selectively highlights 34 makes and models that were a part of the horsepower race of the Fifties. While there are additional cars that could have been included, the intent here is to provide a well-rounded sample, spotlighting each car's successes (and sometimes failures), and to relive however briefly one of the most exciting eras in automotive history.

Everybody's favorite: a '57 Chevy Sport Coupe with fuel injection. More than any other car, it captures the flavor of the "Fabulous Fifties."

5

1954-56 Buick Century

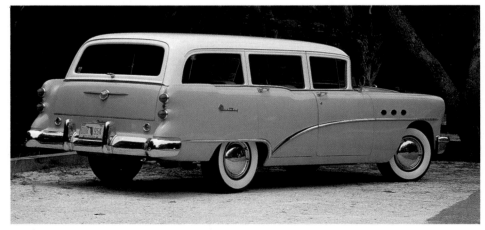

Performance sold cars even in the hard-luck Thirties, especially if it was affordable. Henry Ford proved that with his immensely popular 1932 V-8. The lesson wasn't lost on Harlow Curtice, Buick's general manager beginning in 1933, who okayed a hot new addition for Buick's totally revamped 1936 line: the Series 60 Century.

Named for its near 100-mph top speed, the Century was as neat a combination as peanut butter and jelly: the larger of Buick's two straight eights in a slightly stretched version of the lightweight Special chassis. The results were go-power anyone could appreciate—and extra cash in Buick's bank account. But only for a short time. A more potent Special and a revived Super hurt Century sales after 1937, rendering the line expendable by the time World War II erupted. Because the suspension of civilian manufacturing gave Buick a convenient excuse to forget it, the Century didn't return when peace did.

Things were different by the early Fifties. A horsepower race was raging in Detroit, with overhead-valve V-8s the weapon of choice. Buick had one ready for 1953, and all-new styling for

'54, so that seemed like the perfect time to revive Flint's "factory hot rod." Curtice, now GM president and still following Buick's fortunes, enthusiastically approved.

Though prewar Centurys were always a bit longer and heavier than Specials, they were remembered as the "Special with the Roadmaster engine." The reborn Century was exactly that: the Special's new 122-inch-wheelbase B-body carrying the Roadmaster's 322-cubic-inch "Fireball" V-8. Packing 195 horsepower with manual shift and

8.0:1 compression or 200 horses with optional Dynaflow automatic and an 8.5:1 squeeze—and a four-barrel carburetor—the '54 offered spectacular performance. The result, confirmed by the "car buff" magazines, was the quickest Buick ever: about 11 seconds in the 0-60-mph dash and a 110-mph top end. In the flying-mile contests at Daytona Beach, Florida, in 1954, the fastest Buick averaged 110.425 mph. But as would happen in later years, Chrysler and Cadillac were faster, forcing Buick to settle for fifth place.

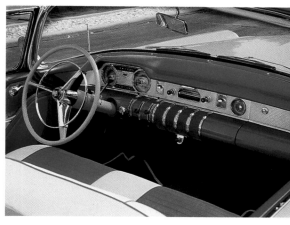

Opposite page: Among the rarest of the Fifties Buick Centurys was the '54 Estate Wagon, a mid-year model that bowed in April 1954. Only 1563 were built at a base price of $3470. That year, Centurys sported three "VentiPorts"—only the top-line Roadmasters got four. *This page:* For 1955, all Buicks featured a new grille and taillights, and Centurys were given four VentiPorts. Horsepower was upped from 195/200 to 236, making 10 second 0-60-mph runs for the lighter models a possibility. Befitting its $2991 price, the convertible came with a luxurious interior. It found 5588 buyers, a far cry from the 80,338 customers who chose the $2601 Riviera hardtop coupe.

The '54 Century lineup started out with a sedan and Riviera hardtop coupe, but a convertible arrived in April to replace the ultra-high-priced '54 Skylark. Bowing with it was the first Century Estate Wagon, sharing all-steel bodywork with the Special. Of course, engineering and Buick's squarish new '54 look, featuring a wrapped Panoramic windshield, were as for other Buick series. Options included power steering and the Skylark's handsome Kelsey-Hayes chrome wire wheels.

Though late introduction held '54

output to 81,982 units, Century zoomed to 158,796 for record-setting '55. Bragging points included an attractive line-wide facelift and 36-41 more horsepower, 236 in all on a 9.0:1 compression ratio. It was a nice jump, but not in the year of the hot Chrysler 300. At Daytona, the Century's best effort in the standing-start and flying miles netted a pair of fourths. A Cadillac and a swift Chevrolet duo won in acceleration, but at least the Century edged the fastest 300. The flying mile saw 300s 1-2, and Cadillac third. The

Century was popular as a stock-car racer in 1954 and even more so in '55, when Buick got its only two wins in NASCAR (National Association for Stock Car Auto Racing) Grand National competition.

Model offerings for '55 expanded to include a two-door sedan and new four-door Riviera hardtop, the former seeing only 280 built, the latter an instant hit. A 0-60-mph dash now averaged about 10 seconds and top speed nudged 115, yet when driven with restraint the Century could approach 20 mpg.

7

1954-56 Buick Century Major Specifications

Engine:	ohv V-8, 322 cid
	(4.00 × 3.20-in. bore × stroke)
1954 8.0:1 c.r., 195 bhp; 8.5:1 c.r., 200 bhp	
1955 236 bhp	**1956** 255 bhp
Transmission:	3-speed manual, 2-speed
	Dynaflow automatic
Suspension, front:	upper and lower A-arms,
	coil springs
Suspension, rear:	live axle, semi-elliptic
	leaf springs
Brakes:	front/rear drums
Wheelbase (in.):	122.0
Weight (lbs):	**1954-55** 3,795-3,995
	1956 3,890-4,080
Top speed (mph):	110-115
0-60 mph (sec):	8.9-11.5
Base price:	$2,490-$3,470
Production:	**1954** 4d sdn 31,919 cvt 2,790
	Riviera 2d htp 45,710
	4d Estate Wagon 1,563
	1955 4d sdn 13,269
	Riviera 4d htp 55,088 cvt 5,588
	Riviera 2d htp 80,338 2d sdn 280
	4d Estate Wagon 4,243
	1956 4d sdn 1 (export)
	Riviera 4d htp 20,891
	Riviera Deluxe 4d htp 35,082
	cvt 4,721 Riviera 2d htp 33,334
	4d Estate Wagon 8,160

Another facelift marked the '56 Buicks. Industry volume was down, but the Century retained its runner-up spot in division sales: 102,189 units, nearly 20,000 ahead of the Super. Improved "Variable-Pitch" Dynaflow returned from '55, though Century two- and four-door sedans didn't. Horsepower escalated again, to a thrilling 255, partly due to higher 9.5:1 compression and header-like exhaust manifolds. A dual-exhaust "Power Kit" with chrome extensions was listed, though it didn't change rated output. Road testers confirmed that the '56 Century was the fastest ever, with many magazines pulling 0-60 in less than 10 seconds for the first time. *Motor Life* seemed to be best at it, quoting a mere 8.9 seconds.

Though the 1954-56 Centurys may not have been the fastest cars on the road, they were among the top performers of their day—and they didn't need special dealer-ordered parts to make them go. These were also the most popular of the muscular '50s Centuries, and prized collectibles today.

The '56 Century lineup consisted of five models, with the convertible (*top and center*) serving as the flagship. Priced at $3306, it showed off a revised grille and mildly reshaped front sheetmetal, as well as new taillights. Note the dual exhausts integrated into the rear bumper. Sporty touches included the fully exposed rear wheels and, on this car, wire wheels. Two-toning and bright colors were in vogue, but those wanting more could order three-tone paint, as on the $3256 Century Estate Wagon (*above*), seen here with the regular hubcaps. Production for 1956 was 4721 ragtops and 8160 wagons.

1957-58 Buick Century

The 1954-56 generation Buick Centurys were hot—and popular. In fact, a total of 342,967 were built, and they helped put Buick into third place in model year production in both 1955 and '56. Needless to say, Buick wasn't about to drop its "banker's hot rod" winner, particularly since the Detroit horsepower wars were still raging and showed no signs of letting up.

Buick had a problem, however: how to follow up on its mid-Fifties success. Management also knew that the '57 Ford and Mercury were to be all-new, as would be the entire Chrysler Corporation line, and sister division's Oldsmobile.

Buick's solution was to retain its existing wheelbases, even though the '57s were to be rebodied on a new X-member "Contour" chassis. Though the styling changes were evolutionary, the new cars looked longer, lower, and heavier—and they were. The four-

door sedan was reinstated in the Century line, while the wagon was shorn of B-posts (making it a four-door hardtop), and retitled Caballero.

Styling was quite conservative—too conservative, many say to this day—but performance was another story. A stroked Fireball V-8 yielded 364 cubic inches and with 10.0:1 compression provided 300 bhp (330 with a high-performance kit) for all but the bottom-line Specials. Despite its added bulk averaging about 200 pounds, the '57 was about the fastest Century yet: 0-60 mph took only about nine seconds, although some sources pegged it closer to 10. The enlarged Century engine also swilled premium gas at the rate of 15 mpg, far less in spirited driving. On a happier note, a new ball-joint suspension, in combination with stiffer shocks, resulted in improved handling and a somewhat less spongy ride.

Alas, quality and engineering woes were catching up with Buick after the heady days of 1954-55, when Buick leapfrogged over Plymouth, copping third place in the sales race for the first time since 1926. Savoring the sweet taste of success, Buick pushed ahead in 1955 to turn out 781,296 automobiles, a hefty 47-percent increase over the year before and a new record for the division. Unfortunately, it was set at the cost of a serious erosion in quality control, not to mention some uncorrected design flaws, such as in the brakes and rear axles. Thus, total division sales slumped 30 percent from

The '57 Buick received an all-new body, though typical Buick styling cues were evident. The $3270 Riviera hardtop coupe attracted 17,029 buyers. It weighed a hefty 4081 pounds, up nearly 200 pounds over the equivalent 1956 model.

1956, but Century's plunged by nearer 40 percent, to 65,966. In addition, Buick lost its third-place industry ranking to a rebounding Plymouth Division.

Aggravated by a deep national recession, the even hulkier, overchromed "B-58" Buicks fared even worse, plummeting 37 percent from 1957, with the Century falling to just 37,558 units. Buick advertising boasted that "No other Buick ever looked like this. There's no other car on the road quite like it—from the Dynastar Grille right back to the twin tower taillights." Buyers agreed, but not as Buick intended, for styling was severely criticized, particularly for the heavy-handed use of chrome trim. Adding insult to injury, the '58 Century was not only slower (averaging 11.2 seconds 0-60) even though it ran with the same 300 horsepower and 10.0:1 compression, but thirstier (less than 10 mpg "economy" in city driving). One of the reasons for the erosion in acceleration and economy was the new Flight-Pitch Dynaflow automatic (later also known as the "triple turbine" transmission), standard on the largest Buicks and optional on lesser models. It relied entirely on hydraulic multiplication throughout the car's speed range, resulting in almost incredible smoothness. On the downside, however, it lacked the quick response of GM's Hydra-Matic, and slippage was such that it proved to be

1957-58 Buick Century Major Specifications

Engine:	ohv V-8, 364 cid (4.125 × 3.40-in. bore × stroke), 10.0:1 c.r., 4-bbl carb, 300 bhp (330 with high-performance kit)
Transmission:	2-speed Dynaflow automatic
Suspension, front:	upper and lower A-arms, coil springs
Suspension, rear:	live axle, torque tube, coil springs
Brakes:	front/rear drums
Wheelbase (in.):	122.0
Weight (lbs):	4,081-4,498
Top speed:	110-115
0-60 (sec):	9.0-11.2
Base price:	$3,234-$3,831
Production:	**1957 4d sdn** 8,075
	Riviera 4d htp 26,589 **cvt** 4,085
	Riviera 2d htp 17,029 **2d sdn** 2 (export)
	Caballero 4d htp wgn 10,186
	1958 4d sdn 7,241
	Riviera 4d htp 15,171 **cvt** 2,588
	Riviera 2d htp 8,100 **2d sdn** 2 (export)
	Caballero 4d htp wgn 4,456

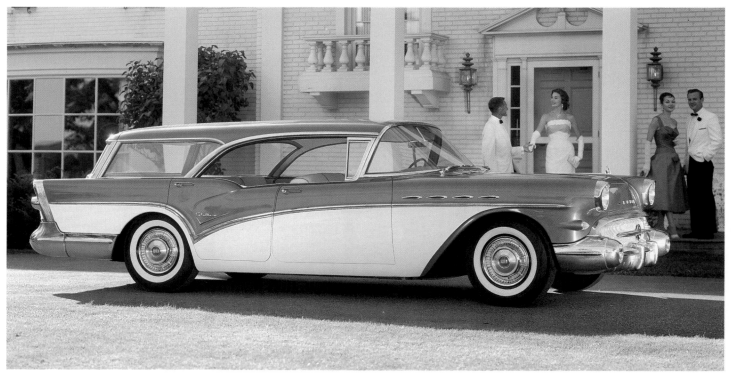

wasteful of fuel. Don Francisco, writing in *Motor Trend*, experienced "extreme slippage somewhere between the engine and the rear wheels. Engine speed went up with the throttle movement, but the car didn't accelerate as it should have."

Despite Buick's problems, the '57 Century was still a very fast car for its time, and the improved suspension and tasteful (if conservative) styling was to its credit. The '58 Century wasn't quite

as fast, though still a mover, and the then-unpopular jukebox styling has many adherents nowadays.

Even so, it was perhaps just as well that Flint retired all of its familiar series names for 1959. The Century name would again return in the Seventies and coast on into the Nineties, but on Buicks that have been nothing like the smooth and speedy mid-Fifties "muscle" models—great American cars one and all.

Like the 1955-56 Centurys, the '57s featured four VentiPorts. A curious styling touch was the three-piece rear window and ribbed roof, as seen on the Riviera coupe (*opposite, top*). Rear-end styling, though chrome-heavy, carried a Buick design theme. The '57 Century wagon (*opposite, bottom and below*), called Caballero, came only as a four-door hardtop. With 10,186 built, it was the most popular Century wagon yet. The '58 Century (*bottom*) received a heavy-handed facelift.

1950-52 Cadillac Series Sixty-One and Sixty-Two

One could ask why the "Standard of the World" has a place among the *Muscle Cars of the '50s*. That's because from 1949 through the mid-1950s Cadillac was nearly as well known for performance as for luxury. In fact, it was one of the first postwar "muscle cars." Cadillacs raced in speed trials, on road courses, and around oval tracks, all with success. And Cadillac engines were immensely popular with the hot-rod and race-car builders of the day. One of the notable examples was the Cadillac-Allard sports car, an Anglo-American hybrid.

To Cadillac, racing wasn't the point—domination of the American luxury-car market was. One means to that end was the pioneering overhead-valve V-8 it introduced for 1949, succeeding its venerable 346-cid L-head V-8. Developed by Edward N.

Cole, Harry F. Barr, and division chief engineer Jack Gordon, this light, efficient oversquare unit—along with Oldsmobile's '49 V-8—set an industry standard for all Detroit V-8s to come. Reversing a long-time industry practice, this short-stroke 331.1-cubic inch powerplant reduced piston travel and therefore wear. The compression ratio was 7.5:1 (previously 7.25:1), and there was potential to go as high as 12.0:1 on super-high octane fuels that never materialized.

The Caddy V-8 weighed about 200 pounds less than the old long-stroker, and was even marginally lighter than the Olds V-8. Features included ample block space for cylinder enlargement, wedge-shaped combustion chambers, and advanced "slipper" pistons. The last traveled low between the crankshaft counterweights to permit short

connecting rods for reduced reciprocating mass. With a two-barrel carb, horsepower came to 160 to tie Packard for the lead. *Motor Trend* observed a "noticeable improvement in acceleration performance" and said that "the average user should get about two miles per gallon better mileage" and increased durability.

Road test magazines were few in 1949, but Tom McCahill reported in *Mechanix Illustrated* that "With this engine, Cadillac, despite its large size, outperforms just about every car being made." He backed that up by posting a 0-60-mph romp of 12.1 seconds and a top speed of around 105 mph. No other car he tested that year did better, and an impressed *Motor Trend* named the '49 Cadillac its first "Car of the Year."

Thus, by 1950 the "Standard of the World" had also become the perform-

The restyled 1950 Cadillac featured a new grille and one-piece windshield (*left*), plus a simulated rear-fender air scoop and its now traditional tailfin design (*above*). Inside was an appropriately chromey dashboard with a 110-mph speedometer (*below*). High-grade materials were used throughout. The Series Sixty-Two Coupe de Ville hardtop enjoyed a production run of 4507 units.

ance standard of America. The aircraft-inspired tailfinned styling ushered in during 1948 at once made Cadillac distinctive and recognizable, and the '49 Coupe de Ville was one of the industry's first hardtop convertibles. The basic styling theme conjured up by Harley Earl, Bill Mitchell, and Art Ross was generally left alone, though made heavier-looking for 1950. The fabled "dollar grin" announced a ponderous, chrome-swathed land yacht, with the sharkfin taillights still defining the rear. A dummy scoop at the leading edge of the rear fenders became a Cadillac hallmark in 1950. The '51s were identified by small auxiliary grilles

under the headlamps; the 50th Anniversary '52s sported a winged badge in that spot. In 1950-51, Cadillac built an unprecedented 100,000 units annually, and by 1952 Cadillac commanded about two-thirds of the luxury market.

Despite its size and weight, the 1950-52 Caddy was no wallowing pig. The relatively light Sixty-Two clocked 0-60 mph in the 12-second range, and better performance could be had by careful tuning. Amazingly, a 1950 Cadillac Sixty-One coupe driven by Sam and Miles Collier finished 10th overall at the world's greatest road race, Le Mans—a performance never matched by any other luxury make. Briggs Cunningham also raced a streamlined Cadillac special that year—dubbed *Le Monstre* by the French—which was even faster, but he lost top gear and slid in the corners, finishing 11th.

Granted, these were specially prepared cars, but even off the floor Caddys were serious performers. A lightweight Sixty-One, still available with a stick shift in 1950-51, would pace a Jaguar XK-120 to 90 mph and the only thing quicker in those days was perhaps the Olds 88. Even a '52 Sixty-Two sedan with Hydra-Matic, as tested by *Motor Trend*, did 0-60 in 13.2 seconds and topped out at 115.4 mph. *MT*, again impressed, gave Cadillac its 1952 Engineering Achievement Award.

The secret to Cadillac's success in 1950-52 was to concentrate on a relative handful of models and to build them extremely well and with the finest materials. The big gun was always the Sixty-Two four-door sedan, which usually sold around 50,000 units per year, but the rarer Sixty-One, especially with stick shift, was the one performance buffs admired.

1950-52 Cadillac Series Sixty-One and Sixty-Two Major Specifications

Engine:	ohv V-8, 331.1 cid (3.81 × 3.63-in. bore × stroke)
1950-51	7.5:1 c.r., 2-bbl carb, 160 bhp
1952	4-bbl carb, 190 bhp
Transmission:	1950-51 3-speed manual
	1950-52 4-speed Hydra-Matic automatic
Suspension, front:	upper and lower A-arms, coil springs
Suspension, rear:	live axle, semi-elliptic leaf springs
Brakes:	front/rear drums
Wheelbase (in.):	**Series 61** 122.0
	Series 62 126.0
Weight (lbs):	3,822-4,416
Top speed (mph):	100-115
0-60 mph (sec):	12.1-14.0
Base price:	$2,761-$4,153
Production:	**1950** Series 61 cpe 11,839
	4d sdn 14,931
	Series 62 4d sdn 41,890 cpe 6,434
	Coupe de Ville htp cpe 4,507 cvt 6,986
	1951 Series 61 cpe 2,400 4d sdn 2,300
	Series 62 4d sdn 55,352 coupe 10,132
	Coupe de Ville htp cpe 10,241 cvt 6,117
	1952 Series 62 4d sdn 42,625 cpe 10,065
	Coupe de Ville htp cpe 11,165 cvt 6,400

The 1951 Cadillac, all Series Sixty-Two models shown here, was little changed, though sharp eyes could detect the angled front bumper guards and the "waffle pattern" trim beneath the headlights. Horsepower of the overhead-valve V-8 remained at 160, though a four-barrel carburetor would up that to 190 horses in 1952. The '51 Coupe de Ville, seen with the side windows up and down (*center and bottom*), sold for $3843 and weighed in at 4156 pounds. Production more than doubled to 10,241 units. Sun worshippers had to pay $3987 to indulge themselves (*top*), and 6117 convertible buyers did exactly that. The '51 soft top's heft was considerable: 4377 pounds.

1955-56 Cadillac Eldorado

The 1936 Century combined Buick's largest engine and smallest chassis (somewhat modified) to create its legendary "banker's hot rod." Beginning in 1949, Cadillac filled that role with a modern overhead V-8 powering its lighter Series Sixty-One models. But though Cadillacs soon got bigger and heavier, the "Standard of the World" had a trick up its sleeve— the Eldorado.

In debut 1953, the Eldo was a $7750 ultra-luxury, limited-volume convertible that weighed 300-600 pounds more than other Series Sixty-Two models, but ran with the same 210-bhp V-8. With 8.25:1 compression, it was

Up front, the '55 Eldorado looked like other Caddys, but it was set apart from the Series Sixty-Two convertible by its unique "sharkfin" rear end, jet-tube taillights, beltline bright metal appliqués, and "Sabre Spoke" wheel covers.

1955-56 Cadillac Eldorado Major Specifications

Engine:	ohv V-8, 2 4-bbl carbs
1955	331 cid (3.81 × 3.63-in. bore × stroke), 9.0:1 c.r., 270 bhp
1956	365 cid (4.00 × 3.63 in.), 9.75:1 c.r., 305 bhp
Transmission:	4-speed Hydra-Matic automatic
Suspension, front:	upper and lower A-arms, coil springs
Suspension, rear:	live axle, semi-elliptic leaf springs
Brakes:	front/rear drums
Wheelbase (in.):	129.0
Weight (lbs):	4,665-4,810
Top speed (mph):	110-115
0-60 mph (sec):	11.0-12.0
Base price:	$6,286-$6,556
Production:	**1955** cvt 3,950
	1956 Biarritz cvt 2,150
	Seville htp cpe 3,900

tops in the horsepower race, but the Eldorado wasn't that year's fastest Caddy. The '54 version—larger and considerably cheaper at $5738—cut the weight penalty to just 205 pounds more than the Sixty-Two ragtop while horsepower jumped to 230.

Cadillac had usually been a contender in the Speed Week trials at Daytona Beach, but its first outright win came in 1954 when Joe Littlejohn drove a Sixty-Two hardtop to a 76.251-mph average to win the standing-start mile. It even beat back the 235-bhp Chrysler, the industry's horsepower leader. No matter, *Motor Trend* gave its "Performance Car of the Year" award to Cadillac, noting its Daytona victory.

In 1955, the Eldorado strutted a unique "sharkfin" tail end, two years ahead of Chrysler's towering fins. Taillights and backup lamps were carried underneath the fins in little round pods. On the body sides, the '55 flashed new "Sabre Spoke" wheel covers, bright metal appliqués along the beltline under the windows, and arched rear wheel openings, sans skirts.

More important to enthusiasts was another Eldorado feature begun in 1955: higher-than-normal performance from the big-block 331-cubic-inch V-8. While other Cadillacs boasted a hearty 250 horsepower—ahead of Lincoln's 225 and equal to the Chrysler New Yorker's Hemi—Eldorados rated 270 horses at 4800 rpm, thanks to twin Carter or Rochester four-barrel carbs and 9.0:1 compression. This setup was optional on other Caddys.

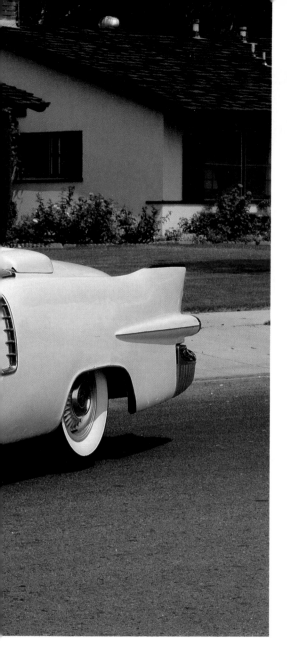

The '56 Eldorado featured a refined grille treatment, and the convertible (*above*) was joined by a new hardtop coupe. Both received distinctive names for 1956: Biarritz for the ragtop, Seville for the closed model. Cadillac had given the '55 Eldo 20 horsepower more than its other models—270 versus 250—and did the same for 1956: 305 horses compared to 285. The increased base horsepower came compliments of a bore job that upped displacement to 365 cubic inches, while the Eldo's extra output was provided by dual four-barrel carbs. It was needed, too, as Eldo road-ready weights were pushing the two-and-a-half-ton mark. Still, 0-60 mph came up in about 11 seconds. Output in 1956: Biarritz, 2150; Seville, 3900.

Most speed fans remember 1955 as the year the 300-bhp Chrysler 300 devastated racing, especially with a record 126.580-mph flying-mile at Daytona Beach. But few remember that Cadillac was again the fastest in acceleration, setting a record mark of 80.428 mph at the hands of Littlejohn. That was better than two mph faster than runner-up Chevrolet. The flying-mile winner could only manage fifth in the standing-start mile, better than 3½ mph off Littlejohn's pace.

In 1956, when Cadillac bored its V-8 to 365 cubic inches, the Eldorado still had an extra 20 horses, now an exhilarating 305 at 4700 rpm on 9.75:1 compression. Not only that, a stump-pulling 400 lbs/ft torque was available on demand. This translated into a small edge in acceleration for the new-for-'56 Eldorado Seville hardtop over the 220-pounds-lighter Sixty-Two hardtop, but didn't make any apparent difference in top speed.

Car magazines didn't road test the 1955-56 Eldorados—Cadillac didn't exactly pass them around—but the models they did test gave a good indication of the Eldo's abilities. *Motor Life* put a '54 Sixty-Two sedan through its paces, and even with 400 pounds of optional equipment it did 0-60 mph in 11.4 seconds, the quarter-mile in 18.5, and topped out at 117.1 mph. It also averaged 17.4 mpg in mixed city-country driving. A year later, *ML* wrung out a '55 Sixty Special; it zipped from 0-60 in 11.2 seconds, ran the quarter in

19.0, and mustered 116 mph flat out. It yielded 16.5 mpg at a steady 60 mph. *Motor Life* noted that "just over 10 seconds are claimed" for the 0-60 time of the '56 Cadillac, and *Motorsport* pretty much backed that up by doing it in 10.7 seconds in a Sixty Special, "a 5,000 pound automobile."

Eldorado production nearly doubled to 3950 units for 1955, and shot up another 50 percent in '56—the year the Eldo broke the 5000 mark. Not surprisingly, the Seville outsold the convertible, now called Biarritz, by 3900 units to 2150. In 1956, another component of the Eldorado marketing plan clicked into place: once established and desirable, up went the price! Even in those inflationless times, Eldorado prices were galloping. The '55 convertible ($6286) listed at $548 more than the '54; in 1956 the Biarritz rose an additional $270—and the Seville cost exactly the same even though it surely cost less to build.

But that was the point. Cadillac was building an exclusive banker's hot rod—for presidents running the most prestigious institutions—to enhance its image. The extra power of the 1955-56 Eldorados did just that. Better yet, the luxury-laden Eldos could nose out (or at least keep pace with) the lighter Cadillacs. And that was going some, for *Motor Life* stated in 1955 that "Cadillac is probably the fastest volume production car on the road, with accelerating ability exceeded only by its top speed."

1957-58 Cadillac Eldorado

The Eldorado entered 1957 in the same mode as before: powerful, flashy, and unique. Still, Cadillac's flagship saw hard times in the late Fifties recession, as did just about every other Detroit glamour boat—along with the industry as a whole. Cadillac suffered less than most, but the Eldorados—Biarritz convertible and Seville hardtop—fell off by heavy margins. Perhaps that's because they didn't seem as special as before, and though each retained its tail-finned individuality, both were upstaged by the *grand luxe* Eldorado Brougham. Also, Eldo prices took big jumps upward to $7286 in 1957 and $7500 in '58, really serious money then.

By this time, Cadillac was out of racing, though the four-barrel 365 V-8 saw compression raised to 10.0:1 and horsepower upped 15 to an even 300. Better yet, the flagship Biarritz and Seville again featured twin four-barrel Carter carbs, good for 325 bhp at 4800 rpm and 400 lbs/ft torque.

Alas, weight continued creeping upward: Seville, 4810 pounds (up 145),

Biarritz, 4930 (up 50). Thus, either Eldo with a full tank and driver aboard tipped the scales at two and a half tons. The bottom line was that, according to contemporary road tests, performance remained about the same as in recent years. *Motor Life*, reporting on a Series Sixty-Two Sedan de Ville, obtained 0-30 and 0-60 times of 4.0 and 10.9 seconds. Since it weighed 155 pounds more, the Seville needed the extra 25 horses to keep pace. It took *Motor Trend* 12.4 seconds to reach 60 mph in a 5140-pound Sixty Special with an "economy" 3.07:1 rear axle.

Remaining technically within the Sixty-Two series, the Biarritz/Seville shared its 129.5-inch wheelbase. However, the tapered, rounded tail sprouting tall, flashy sharkfins made the Eldos unique. So did Sabre Spoke wheel covers, and sharp-eyed observers noted there was no hood ornament. Broad, bright-metal lower rear-fender appliqués were revived from '54, and as always Eldorados sported almost fully exposed rear wheels. Up front, they

smiled as brightly as other Caddys, but chromy, leather swathed interiors further set them apart. Cadillac, it might be noted, built four '57 Seville *four*-door hardtops, specially prepared for show purposes and/or trial marketing.

Biarritz/Seville output skidded from 6050 in 1956 to 3900 for '57, but the facelifted '58—with a wider and chromier grin and quad headlights—fared even worse: 1670 units. An optional—and troublesome—air suspension system appeared, but a new trailing-arm four-link coil rear suspension resulted in less sway, reduced rear-end breakaway, and easier correction. The '58s still ran with the four-barrel 365 V-8, now with 10.25:1 compression and 310 bhp. Eldorados, meanwhile, boasted triple Rochester two-barrel carbs, upping the ante to 335 horses at 4800 rpm and a prodigious 405 lbs/ft torque at 3400 rpm. Since weight was up another 100 pounds—5070 for the Biarritz—performance was again little changed. *Motor Trend* romped from 0-30 in 3.9 seconds and 0-60 in 11.7 in the

Though the '57 Cadillacs were all-new, there was no mistaking them for anything else. Eldorados again differed from the other models primarily at the rear, where they sported their own rounded sheetmetal and towering rear-slanted fins. A '57 Seville hardtop (*opposite*) listed at a hefty $7286, but the buyer received a sumptuous interior (*left*) and a long list of standard equipment. Curiously, the Biarritz ragtop (*below*) also sold at $7286. Output of the two models totaled 3900 units. Though the '58 Eldo (*bottom*) looked the same from the back, it wore a glitzy new grille and ran with 335 horses fed by triple two-barrel carbs.

1957-58 Cadillac Eldorado Major Specifications

Engine:	ohv V-8, 365 cid (4.00 × 3.63-in. bore × stroke)
	1957 10.0:1 c.r., 2 4-bbl carbs, 325 bhp
	1958 10.25:1 c.r., 3 2-bbl carbs, 335 bhp
Transmission:	four-speed Dual Range Hydra-Matic
Suspension, front:	independent, coil springs, tube shocks **1958** central compressor and accumulator, self-leveling with air bags opt.
Suspension, rear:	live axle, coil springs, tube shocks **1958** central compressor and accumulator, self-leveling, with four-link rear suspension and air bags
Brakes:	power assisted front/rear drums
Wheelbase (in.):	129.5
Weight (lbs):	4,810-5,070
Top speed (mph):	115-120
0-60 mph (sec):	11.0-12.0
Base price:	$7,286-$7,500
Production:	**1957 Biarritz** cvt cpe 1,800
	Seville htp cpe 2,100 (plus 4 Seville htp sdns built experimentally)
	1958 Biarritz cvt cpe 815
	Seville htp cpe 855

310-bhp Coupe de Ville, while a Sedan de Ville tested by *Popular Mechanics, Car Life,* and *Motor Life* did 0-60 in 12.4, 11.5, and 11 seconds flat.

These were still excellent figures, but at this point Cadillac seemed far more interested in out-and-out luxury and flash. And 1959 would see the flashiest Caddys of all time, plus 390-cid, 345-bhp Eldorados that maintained about the same level of performance. Even so, luxury would henceforth be the key-note at Cadillac.

1955 Chevrolet V-8

Chevrolet's *red-hot* hill-flatteners !
162 H.P. V8 · 180 H.P. V8

See that line hit mountain yonder?

You can lean it out. flat as a flounder . . . and easy as whistling!

Just point one of Chevrolet's special hill-flatteners at it [either the 162-h.p. "Turbo-Fire V8," or the 180-h.p. "Super Turbo-Fire"] . . . and pull the trigger!

Bar-r-r-r-o-o-o-o-G-O-O-OM!

Mister, you got you a flat mountain!

At least it feels flat. Because those all-out-dynamic V8's gobble up the toughest grades you can inch out. And holler for more. They love to climb, because that's just about the only time the throttle ever comes near the floorboard.

And that's a pity. For here are engines that clog as sweetly at a dip-stroke . . . built to pour out a torrent of pure, vibrationless power. Hip-deep V8's with the shortest stroke in the industry, designed to grip huge breaths of fresh air and transmute it into blazing acceleration.

So most of the time they loaf. Even at the speed limit they just dream along, light and easy as a zephyr, putting out an effortless fraction of their strength.

You don't have to be an engineer to know that these are the tamest-running V8's you ever piloted. Just drop in at your Chevrolet dealer's, point the nose at the nearest hill, and feather the throttle open. Those V8's can do their own talking . . . and nobody argues with them!

SEE YOUR CHEVROLET DEALER
Optional at extra cost.

motoramic **CHEVROLET** *Stealing the thunder from the high-priced cars with the most modern V8 on the road!*

Don't argue with *this* baby!" warned one '55 Chevy ad. With plenty to crow about, Chevrolet quickly spread the news about its all-new lineup highlighted by attractive "Motoramic" styling and a potent new "Turbo-Fire" V-8. The '55 Chevy was one of those happy—and rare—cars whose whole exceeded the sum of its parts. And as the most exciting car ever to wear the "bowtie" badge, it lived up to its billing: "New Look! New Life! New Everything!"

The styling was both clean and boxy, altogether sleeker and crisper than the stodgy 1953-54 models despite the unchanged 115-inch wheelbase. Features included 2.5-inch lower height (six inches for wagons), "Sweep Sight" wraparound windshield, a rakish beltline dip, taillamps that jutted out slightly from the rear fenders, flashy two-toning, and a Ferrari-like eggcrate grille.

The '55 Chevy also boasted a new chassis and drivetrain developed with weight-saving in mind. The frame was 18 percent lighter and 50 percent stiffer, with less unsprung weight and more widely spaced siderails for better stability. Mechanical features em-

braced Hotchkiss drive, Salisbury-type rear axle, ball-joint front suspension, nine-inch-longer rear leaf springs, recirculating ball-and-nut steering, 11-inch "Jumbo Drum" brakes, and 12-volt electrics.

Chevy still offered its faithful "Stovebolt" six, but the big news was the new 265-cubic-inch V-8, which was 30 percent more powerful and 40 pounds lighter than the six. It arrived with an 8.0:1 compression ratio and 162 horsepower with a two-barrel carburetor. The 90-degree short-stroke engine featured five main bearings, hollow pushrods, valve guides integral with the cylinder heads, short connecting rods, slipper-type "autothermic" aluminum pistons, stamped-metal rocker arms, and a precision-cast cylinder block.

Backing up Chevy's claim that the V-8 was "a *red-hot* hill flattener" was a "Super Turbo-Fire" Power Pack version. Optional for all but wagons, it boasted a smashing 180 bhp via dual exhausts and a Rochester four-barrel carb. Then late in the model year an ad in *Motor Trend* announced: "SPECIAL: Added power for the Chevrolet 'Super

1955 Chevrolet V-8 Major Specifications	
Engine:	ohv V-8, 265 cid (3.75 × 3.00-in. bore × stroke), 162 bhp, 180 bhp with Power Pack, 195 bhp with Special Power Kit
Transmission:	3-speed manual; Touch-Down Overdrive or 2-speed Powerglide automatic opt.
Suspension, front:	upper and lower A-arms, coil springs, tube shocks
Suspension, rear:	live axle, longitudinal semi-elliptic leaf springs, tube shocks
Brakes:	front/rear drums
Wheelbase (in.):	115.0
Weight (lbs):	3,070-3,370
Top speed (mph):	98-115
0-60 mph (sec):	9.7-11.4
Base price (V-8):	$1,692-$2,571
Production (Six & V-8):	One-Fifty 2d sdn 66,416 4d sdn 29,898 2d utility sdn 11,196 Handyman 4d wgn 17,936
	Two-Ten 2d sdn 249,105 4d sdn 317,724 Townsman 4d wgn 82,303 Delray 2d sdn 115,584 Handyman 2d wgn 28,918 Sport Coupe 2d htp 11,675
	Bel Air 2d sdn 168,313 4d sdn 345,372 Beauville 4d wgn 24,313 cvt 41,292 Sport Coupe 2d htp 185,562 Nomad 2d wgn 8,386

Turbo-Fire' V-8—the new 195-h.p. Special Power Kit now available at extra cost on special order." Intended primarily for racing, this engine was the Power Pack with a Corvette camshaft and valve springs. Transmission choices consisted of a three-speed manual (with 3.70:1 rear axle), "Touch-Down" overdrive (4.11:1 gearing), and two-speed Powerglide automatic (3.55:1 gearing). Stick shift V-8s used mechanical valve lifters; Powerglide cars got hydraulics.

Hot rodders quickly dubbed Chevy's high-revving V-8 "The Hot One," while road testers greeted the new car with near universal acclaim. Floyd Clymer reported in *Popular Mechanics* that his Powerglide-equipped Bel Air topped 108 mph; *Motor Trend*'s 180-bhp car did 0-60 in 11.4 seconds, the quarter-mile in 18.4 seconds, and the 50-80-mph passing spurt in 12.9 seconds. *Road & Track* got the best numbers with the stick-overdrive/Power Pack combo in a light Two-Ten two-door: 9.7 seconds 0-60, 17.2 seconds in the quarter-mile. Fuel economy? A creditable 18-22 miles per gallon.

Such formidable performance led to competition, beginning with the Daytona Speed Weeks in February. Jack Radtke finished 10th overall in the traditional road-and-beach race against Buicks, Oldsmobiles, and Chrysler 300s, while other Chevys took the top four spots in class and eight of the first 11 positions. In the two-way measured mile, three Chevys were among the five fastest cars in the 250-299 cid class. "Smokey" Yunich entered a V-8 Chevy in NASCAR short-track contests, where it proved unbeatable in the hands of former Hudson Hornet pilot Herb Thomas. It was equally capable in NASCAR's longer Grand National events, with Thomas and Fonty Flock often beating out much larger and more powerful machinery.

Like other automakers, Chevy began issuing heavy-duty "export" parts through key dealers to get its best hardware into racers' hands. It paid off. Thomas won the Southern 500 at Darlington, South Carolina, on Labor Day averaging 92.281 mph, followed by Jim Reed in another Chevy. Tim Flock, Fonty's brother, was third in a Chrysler 300, but Chevy took seven of the first 10 places. October brought a repeat per-

Opposite page: Chevy's 162- and 180-horse Turbo-Fire V-8s were good enough to be advertised (*bottom*) as "red-hot hill-flatteners!" And indeed, with relatively low curb weights, the new Chevys could out accelerate many much more powerful and expensive cars. That was because of "Big-bore V8's with the shortest stroke in the industry, designed to gulp huge breaths of fresh air and transmute it into blazing acceleration." Slick styling enticed buyers, too. The '55 Bel Air Sport Coupe (*top*), priced at $2067, saw output reach 185,562 units. *This page*: Fun-in-the-sun types, 41,292 of them, chose the Bel Air ragtop. Its base price was $2206.

formance at Charlotte, and Chevy ran 1-2 at Atlanta. Meanwhile, another ex-Hudson driver, Marshall Teague, began dominating the American Automobile Association (AAA) circuit. And symbolizing Chevy's new prowess, a Bel Air convertible served as the Official Pace Car for the '55 Indy 500. In all, 1955 was the greatest competition year for a low-price make in years.

And 1955 would be only the opening chapter in the performance logbook of "The Hot One" from "USA-1."

1956 Chevrolet V-8

"The Hot One's Even Hotter!" boasted one '56 Chevy ad. After a rousing 1955, Chevrolet followed up with more style, more refinements, and more power—all "to make the going sweeter."

In lieu of the expected minor facelift, the '56 strutted new lower sheetmetal save doors and decklid, a sparkling full-width grille, extended rear fenders, revised taillights, rounder wheel openings, additional bodyside chrome, and bolder two-toning. The '56 looked a bit more imposing—and more Cadillac-like than ever. The lineup, similar to 1955, embraced new Two-Ten and Bel Air Sport Sedan four-door hardtops, which proved quite popular.

The '56 Chevy also received a number of engineering refinements. Among them were longer, lower-rate front coil springs to reduce nosedive in hard braking and increased caster angle for easier steering. At the rear, the leaf springs resided two inches further outboard for better cornering stability, while wider hangers with more rubber better resisted compression from lateral axle motion. Enthusiastic drivers ordered the newly optional six-

leaf (versus five-leaf) springs to enhance handling.

With the "horsepower race" raging, "go" again vied with "show" for customer attention. "Loves to Go…And Looks It!" said one ad, and Chevy proved its "Go" early. On Labor Day 1955, a disguised Bel Air Sport Sedan charged up Pikes Peak in 17 minutes, 24.05 seconds, setting a new American stock-sedan record—two minutes, three seconds faster than the previous best. Driven and prepared by Corvette engineering wizard Zora Arkus-Duntov, this car charged skyward with the new "Super Turbo-Fire" V-8, optional on any '56 Chevy. Basically, it was the existing 265 with a special Power Pack kit comprising specific intake manifold, higher-lift cam, dual exhausts, four-barrel carb, and higher 9.25:1 compression. Output: 205 horsepower at 4600 rpm and 234 lbs/ft torque. Chevy trumpeted the victory, bragging that "No other car has ever gone so high so fast—so safely."

But that was only the beginning. Ford upped the power ante at mid-year, so Chevy made the top Corvette engine an across-the-board option.

With mechanical instead of hydraulic lifters, the first of the famous "Duntov" cams, plus twin four-barrel carbs, lightweight valves, and larger intake and exhaust passages, it belted out 225 lively horses at 5200 rpm.

Even workaday V-8s were a bit more potent for '56, with wilder cam profiles for all save the 162-bhp mill with manual shift. The base Powerglide V-8 produced 170 bhp at 4400 rpm. All V-8s could be ordered with extra-cost full-flow—instead of bypass type—oil filters and dual exhausts became available for wagons. Other features: improved warmup and driveability via a revised automatic choke (a mid-1955 running change), larger passages for the intake manifold heat riser, a more deeply grooved throttle body on four-barrel carbs, "hotter" four-rib spark plugs, and a beefier clutch for Super Turbo-Fire V-8s. For those who cared, the newly named "Blue Flame 140" six trotted with that many horses and 210 lbs/ft torque.

Motor Trend's Jim Lodge lauded the handling, noting that "Recovery from bumps, dips, and potholes is rapid, non-

1956 Chevrolet V-8 Major Specifications

Engine:	ohv V-8, 265 cid (3.75 × 3.00-in. bore × stroke): 162/170 bhp (manual/Powerglide), 205 bhp with Power Pack, 225 bhp with Corvette option
Transmission:	3-speed manual; Touch-Down Overdrive or 2-speed Powerglide opt.
Suspension, front:	upper and lower A-arms, coil springs, tube shocks
Suspension, rear:	live axle, longitudinal semi-elliptic leaf springs, tube shocks
Brakes:	front/rear drums
Wheelbase (in.):	115.0
Weight (lbs):	3,117-3,506
Top speed (mph):	100-115
0-60 mph (sec):	8.9-12.0
Base price (V-8):	$1,833-$2,707

Production (Six & V-8):	One-Fifty 2d	
sdn 82,384	4d sdn 51,544	
2d utility sdn 9,879		
Handyman 2d wgn 13,487		
Two-Ten 2d sdn 205,545	4d sdn 283,125	
Townsman 4d wgn 113,656		
Sport Sedan 4d htp 20,021		
Beauville 4d wgn 17,988		
Delray 2d sdn 56,382		
Handyman 2d wgn 22,038		
Sport Coupe 2d htp 18,616		
Bel Air 2d sdn 104,849	4d sdn 269,798	
Sport Sedan 4d htp 103,602		
Beauville 4d wgn 13,279	cvt 41,268	
Sport Coupe 2d htp 128,382		

jarring in most cases, and free from wallowing or pitching." And nobody complained about performance. The basic 170-bhp/Powerglide combo zipped from 0-60 mph in 11.9 seconds and topped 98 mph for *Motor Life*. The 205-bhp version recorded an impressive 8.9 seconds and 108.7 mph, though *Motor Trend*'s 205-bhp/Powerglide Chevy was timed at 10.7 seconds, 109.1 mph flat out, and 18.3 seconds and 76 mph in the quarter-mile. Ordering a lighter 205-bhp/stick-shift Two-Ten two-door, *Road & Track* managed 0-60 in nine seconds flat, 111 at top end, and 16.6 seconds and 80 mph in the standing quarter. *Motor Life* stated that the '56 Power Pack knocked 0.9 second from the '55 Power Pack's 12.9-second time in the 50-80 mph passing test.

The 225-horse version was faster still. Tom McCahill, of *Mechanix Illustrated*, wrote: "Chevrolet has come up with a poor man's Ferrari....Here's an engine that can wind up tighter than the E string on an East Laplander's mandolin...well beyond 6000 rpm without blowing up like a pigeon egg in a shotgun barrel." McCahill judged Chevy

The '56 Chevrolet

It looks high priced—but it's the new Chevrolet "Two-Ten" 4-Door Sedan.

For sooner and safer arrivals!

It's so nimble and quick on the road...

HOT ONE'S EVEN HOTTER

CHEVROLET

the year's "best performance buy in the world," while *ML* said it gave "the best performance per dollar." Even *R&T* gushed that "The surge of power (actually torque) is there at all times...."

Competition results were equally satisfying. Smokey Yunick returned to Darlington's 24-hour enduro with four '56s; one finished at an average 101.58 mph, beating Chrysler's previous U.S. production-car record by 11.69 mph. In July, three cars prepared by Vince Piggins, recruited from fast-fading Hudson, contested the annual Pikes Peak hillclimb, with Chevys com-

"The Hot One's Even Hotter!" boasted Chevy ads in 1956 (*left*). It was, even though the V-8 remained at 265 cubic inches. In 1955, horsepower ratings had been 162, 180, and late in the year, 195. In 1956, it was 162, 170, 205, and 225 horses, the last with the first of the famous "Duntov" cams and twin four-barrel carbs. The cars housing these V-8s looked more Cadillac-like, highlighted by a full-width chromey grille. Among the models offered were the $2344 Bel Air convertible (*opposite*), $2176 Bel Air Sport Coupe (*this page, top*), and the $2025 Bel Air two-door sedan (*above*).

ing in 1-2-5-6-10. Better yet, winner Jerry Unser, Jr., leaped to the summit in 16 minutes, 8 seconds, 1:16 faster than Duntov's late-'55 showing.

In 1956, Chevy offered dealers a "special kit" to tie in with local stock car races, with posters asking people to "Traffic test the short track champ!" Indeed, NASCAR short-track (less than a half-mile length) standings were grist for the mill. In 1955, Chevy won this classification by a huge margin: 668 points to Oldsmobile's 195, Hudson's 184, Dodge's 176, and Ford's 165. And through April 28, 1956, Chevy was the only make in triple digits: 226 points to second-place Ford's 91.

Truly, the "Hot One" *was* even hotter in 1956.

1957 Chevrolet 283 V-8

Chevy hyped its '57s as "Sweet, Smooth, and Sassy!" And indeed, the new styling *was* sweet, the new Turboglide automatic was truly smooth, and the fuel-injected 283 V-8 was *very* sassy. Meanwhile, the bigger and more powerful '57 Fords and Plymouths boasted dashingly attractive all-new styling. Chevy, making do with a heavy facelift of its 1955 bodyshell, shouted that "This is the car that's fresher and friskier from its own special look to its new Ramjet fuel injection."

That "special" '57 look was pleasingly different than in 1955-56 and—if not the last word in style—attractive enough. Designer Carl Renner later observed that the goal was to make the '57 look like a "little Cadillac," so Chevy talked up its "BOLD 'BIG CAR' STYLING!" Features included a massive new bumper/grille, lowered hood sporting twin windsplits, full-length bodyside trim with brushed aluminum inserts on Bel Airs, and modest blade fins atop half-moon taillights.

But "sassy" was where Chevy really scored for '57. That's because of the undeniable performance of the newly enlarged 283-cubic-inch V-8 and the presumed historical significance of the top 283-horsepower version with "Ramjet" fuel injection (also available on the Corvette). This prompted Chevy to claim an industry first in a now-famous ad reading "1 h.p. per cubic inch." That was because of "the *extra* efficiency of Chevrolet's advanced valve gear, free-breathing manifolding and ultra-short stroke." True, but in 1956 Chrysler had already coaxed 355 horses from its 354-cid Hemi for the 300-B, and the '57 DeSoto Adventurer's 345-cid Hemi developed 345 bhp—both without fuel injection. Nor was Chevy alone with fuel injection in 1957-58; Pontiac, Plymouth, Dodge, DeSoto, Chrysler, and—yes—even Rambler had it, though all except Chevy quickly dropped it.

Notably, Chevy offered a "fuelie" on *all* its '57 models—even the lightweight One-Fifty utility sedan. The 140-bhp six and 162-bhp 265 V-8 still performed well, but the half-dozen 283s were far more stimulating. They started with a four-barrel carb, 8.5:1 compression, and 185 bhp at 4600 rpm. Then came a Super Turbo-Fire quintet with 9.5:1 compression on all but the 283-bhp fuelie. The single four-pot version yielded 220 bhp at 4800 rpm. Twin quads boosted that to 245 bhp at 5000 rpm or 270 at 6000 rpm, the former mated to any transmission, the latter with a high-lift cam and close-ratio three-speed stick. Fuel injection outputs were 250 bhp at 5000 rpm or, on 10.5:1 compression, 283 bhp at 6200 rpm. Both used mechanical lifters; the latter was a high-lift-cam/three-speed screamer.

Chevy's other big engineering news for '57 was a second automatic transmission: Turboglide. This was a complex two-speed, five element geared-converter type with three turbines and twin planetary gearsets plus variable-pitch stator and a conventional torque converter pump. Optional on any 283 save the 270- and 283-bhp versions, it was "as smooth as velvet underpants" according to *Mechanix Illustrated*'s Tom McCahill.

"The Hotter One," as *Motor Trend* put it, remained the hottest of the '57 Low-Price Three. Even the base 283/Powerglide combo was capable of 11-second 0-60 acceleration. Walt Woron's 220-bhp/Turboglide car easily topped 100 mph, hit 60 mph from rest in 10.1

'57 CHEVROLET! SWEET, SMOOTH AND SASSY!

Chevy goes 'em all one better for '57 with a daring new departure in design (looks longer and lower, and it is!), exclusive new Triple-Turbine Turboglide automatic drive, a new V8 and a bumper crop of new ideas including fuel injection!

U·S·A

Fuel Injection

Chevy's big news in 1957 was a new 283 V-8 and "Ramjet" fuel injection (*left*). The 265 still offered 162 horsepower, but the 283 had ratings of 185, 220, 245, and 270 with carbs, plus 250 and 283 with FI. The heavily facelifted 1955-56 bodyshell looked more like a Cadillac than ever, and a new Turboglide automatic appeared. Two of the most desired models were the $2299 Bel Air Sport Coupe (*opposite and this page, bottom*) and the $2511 Bel Air soft top (*below*).

1957 Chevrolet 283 V-8 Major Specifications

Engine:	ohv V-8, 283-cid (3.88 × 3.00-in. bore × stroke): 8.5:1 c.r., 4-bbl carb, 185 bhp; 9.5:1 c.r., 4-bbl carb, 220 bhp; 9.5:1 c.r., 2 4-bbl carbs, 245 bhp; 9.5:1 c.r., high-lift cam, 2 4-bbl carbs, 270 bhp; 9.5:1 c.r., FI, 250 bhp; 10.5:1 c.r., high-lift cam, FI, 283 bhp
Transmission:	3-speed manual; Touch-Down Overdrive, 2-speed Powerglide/Turboglide opt.
Suspension, front:	upper and lower A-arms, coil springs, tube shocks
Suspension, rear:	live axle, semi-elliptic leaf springs, tube shocks
Brakes:	front/rear drums
Wheelbase (in.):	115.0
Weight (lbs):	3,159-3,461
Top speed (mph):	100-120
0-60 mph (sec):	8.0-12.0
Base price (V-8):	$1,985-$2,857
Production (Six & V-8):	**One-Fifty 2d** sdn 70,774 4d sdn 52,266 2d utility sdn 8,300 Handyman 2d wgn 14,740 **Two-Ten 2d** sdn 160,090 4d sdn 260,401 Townsman 4d wgn 127,803 Sport Sedan 4d htp 16,178 Beauville 4d wgn 21,083 Delray 2d sdn 25,644 Handyman 2d wgn 17,528 Sport Coupe 2d htp 22,631 **Bel Air 2d** sdn 62,757 4d sdn 254,331 Townsman 4d wgn 27,375 Sport Sedan 4d htp 137,672 cvt 47,652 Sport Coupe 2d htp 166,426

seconds, and scampered from 50-80 mph in 10.0 seconds. *MT* also tested a 270-bhp/Powerglide Bel Air Sport Sedan for a Chevy/Ford/Plymouth showdown, clocking 9.9 seconds 0-60 and 17.5 seconds at 77.5 mph in the quarter-mile. It won every category but one—Plymouth nipped Chevy from 0-45.

Mainly because of the $500 tariff, only 1503 '57 Chevys got Ramjet engines, so few people knew how hot they were. But in the hands of *MT*'s Walt Woron, the 250-bhp/stick-shift 'Vette did 0-60 in a swift 7.2 seconds,

while the 283-bhp flyer topped 134 mph. With the latter engine and suitable gearing—and a 400-pound weight penalty—a standard '57 Chevy two-door might have done 0-60 mph in about 8.0 seconds and 120-125 mph flat out. Partial confirmation was provided in 1976 by classic Chevy dealer Bob Wingate driving an unrestored 283-bhp Bel Air Sport Coupe with the close-ratio three-speed and 3.70:1 gears. Though not timed for 0-60, it ran the quarter-mile in 14.21 to 14.88 seconds with trap speeds of 103.60 to 104.01 mph!

In NASCAR, Chevy took 18 Grand National wins, but this paled against Ford's 27 victories. But tables were turned in 1958 when most Chevy teams continued running with '57s ('58s were bigger and heavier), coming home first 23 times, compared to 16 for runner-up Ford.

Powerful performance, raw stamina, and elegant engineering combined with nostalgic styling, high popularity, and historic impact have elevated the '57s to favored status among the "classic" 1955-57 Chevys. They were the last of a truly special breed.

1958 Chevrolet Impala 348 V-8

Mention "Impala" and most people immediately think "Chevrolet." For the better part of 25 years, the names were virtually synonymous: the most popular model line from America's perennial best-seller—the nation's favorite family car. But in the beginning, Impala meant something very special.

The Impala debuted as the flagship of a 1958 Chevrolet fleet virtually all-new from the ground up. Conceived as a "Bel Air Executive Coupe," it was intended to stretch the make's coverage from the low-price field into the lower reaches of the medium segment, which product planners had concluded would be the biggest growth market of the late '50s. Reflecting that view, the '58s were deliberately bigger and heavier than the agile, spirited 1955-57 Chevys. This is one reason collectors once ignored the '58s, including Impala, but Chevy was only playing catch-up with Ford and Plymouth, which had moved to their "mid-size" platforms the year before.

And in retrospect, the '58 Chevy was generally much improved, with a lot of what buyers wanted. Its new X-member chassis was not only heftier, but delivered a smoother ride, thanks to a 2.5-inch-longer wheelbase and a new four-link rear suspension with coil springs instead of leaf springs. The latter was designed to facilitate installation of "Level Air" suspension, but the air bags were prone to leaks and the option found few takers at $124.

Of far greater interest was a larger V-8 option: the new 348-cubic-inch "Turbo-Thrust" offering 250 standard horsepower, or 280 with optional 9.5:1 compression and three dual-throat carbs, and 315 bhp with 11.0:1 compression, special camshaft, high-speed valve train, and solid lifters. Although originally designed for Chevy trucks, the 348 made any '58 Chevy more lively than it was usually given credit for—perhaps not as fast as a "fuelie" '57, but quick enough to qualify as a "Hot One" nonetheless. A 250-bhp Bel Air hardtop sedan could run 0-60 in a respect-

able 9.9 seconds; *Motor Trend* timed a 280-bhp Impala Sport Coupe at 9.1 seconds, with 16.5 seconds in the standing quarter-mile. These figures were achieved with Turboglide, the new two-speed Chevy automatic that had

'58's real eye-opener is CHEVY!

1958

And that's a fact. You never saw so much sharp engineering, so many advanced ideas, such stunning changes packed into one year's progress. You'll spend hours studying this one and never run out of surprises. For '58, Chevy's new from the point on in—and that means body, suspension, chassis, engines . . . the works! Sure, they're lovely to look at. But come on down and get the real eye-opener, the inside story! . . . Chevrolet Division of General Motors, Detroit 2, Michigan.

CHEVROLET

bowed during 1957 as an alternative to Powerglide. Other alternatives in 1958 included the six and the 283 V-8s, the top two being 250- and 290-bhp fuelies.

Chevy styling had been moving closer to Cadillac's since 1955, and the '58 was the closest yet. Not everyone applauded the new look, but it was at least distinctive—especially the tasteful "gullwing" rear fenders—and far less shiny than this year's Buick and Oldsmobile. Both the Impala convertible—the only one in the line—and Sport Coupe two-door hardtop were set apart from their Bel Air sisters by stainless-steel rocker moldings, special emblems and wheel covers, and dummy "pitchfork" trim (suggesting air scoops) ahead of the rear wheels.

Yet contrary to popular opinion, the first Impala was more than just fancy trim. Both models had longer rear Ford and Plymouth were all-new for '57, so it was Chevy's turn for '58. The new one, billed as "'58's real eye-opener" (opposite, top), was bigger and heavier. Thus, it's hardly surprising that it could be optioned with a larger V-8, a 348 good for 250 bhp with a four-barrel carb, or 280 or 315 horsepower with triple two-barrels. Also new was the Impala hardtop (below) and ragtop (opposite, bottom). Most any model could be had with the fuel-injected 283, and a few were (bottom row).

decks than other '58s, though overall length was the same, and a somewhat different lower body. Interior exclusives ran to brushed-aluminum door-panel appliqué, color-keyed horizontal-strip upholstery, and a pull-down rear armrest below a central radio speaker grille.

With all this, the Impala was a timely hit, enabling Chevy to weather the dulling 1958 recession far better than most Detroit makes. Despite just two body styles, close to 181,500 were

The Impala was given unique rear deck and taillight styling. The $2693 Sport Coupe V-8 (or $2586 six) featured "pitchfork" simulated bodyside vents and a fake extractor vent on the roof. With a 117.5-inch wheelbase and 3459-pound weight, the bigger '58 Impala proved popular: 125,480 Sport Coupes were built for the model run.

sold—fully 15 percent of the division's model year volume—helping Chevy capture a record 30 percent of the U.S. auto market. By contrast, total industry production dropped to 4.5 million from six million the year before.

Encouraged by this success, Chevy expanded Impala offerings to create a new top-line series for 1959. But in doing so it watered down the concept and, except for the high-performance Super Sports of the '60s, future Impalas would be nowhere near as unique.

But collectors have since come to recognize the '58 as the "Hot One" it was. Today, these cars are being gathered in and restored with the same enthusiasm once reserved for the 1955-57s. If not quite as capable, the first Impala is certainly just as nostalgic as the "classic" Chevys—one of the more pleasant symbols of an unforgettable automotive age.

1958 Chevrolet Impala 348 Major Specifications

Engine:	348-cid ohv V-8
	(4.125 × 3.25-in. bore × stroke):
	9.5:1 c.r., 4-bbl carb, 250 bhp;
	9.5:1 c.r., 3 2-bbl carbs, 280 bhp;
	11.0:1 c.r., 3 2-bbl carbs, 315 bhp
Transmission:	3-speed manual;
	close-ratio 3-speed manual,
	overdrive, 2-speed Powerglide or
	Turboglide automatic,
	Corvette-type Powerglide opt.
Suspension, front:	upper and lower
	A-arms, coil springs
Suspension, rear:	4-link live axle,
	coil springs
Brakes:	front/rear drums
Wheelbase (in.):	117.5
Weight (lbs):	3,459-3,523
Top speed (mph):	105-115
0-60 mph (sec):	8.5-10.0
Base price (V-8):	$2,693-$2,841
Production (all engines):	Sport Coupe
2d htp 125,480	cvt 55,989

1956 Chevrolet Corvette

Had it not been for the Ford Thunderbird, there might not be a Corvette today. In early 1955, General Motors was ready to kill off Chevrolet's fiberglass-bodied two-seater, which since its 1953 debut hadn't made much of an impression on America's sports-car market. But Dearborn's "personal" two-seater was a challenge GM couldn't let go unanswered, so the 'Vette was granted a stay of execution.

The reprieve brought a renaissance. With the all-new second-generation design of 1956-57, Chevy could at last rightfully proclaim the Corvette "America's only true sports car"—as indeed it did. Compared to its slabsided predecessor, the '56 was stunning with new front and rear styling and bodyside "coves"—sexy, low-slung, and distinctly American. Its only questionable elements were phony front-fender air scoops, dummy knock-off hubs, and a dash with more flash than function. The '56 was also more civilized, featuring new seats, roll-up windows (no more clumsy side curtains), and an optional lift-off hard top.

Beneath this finery was a chassis heavily reworked by engineering wizard Zora Arkus-Duntov. Without upsetting the '55's near-equal front/rear weight distribution (52/48 percent), he tightened up both steering response and handling. Understeer

The '56 Corvette maintained the general shape and 102-inch wheelbase of the 1953-55 models, but it was really an almost all-new car. Front and rear styling was updated, and the new bodyside "coves" contributed to a sexy, low-slung, distinctly American look—all for $3149.

was still a tad excessive and the brakes faded under extreme use, but the 'Vette was now as quick through turns as it was on straights.

And quick it was. Chevy's superb 265-cubic-inch V-8, an option fitted to all but six of the '55s, now came standard. With a four-barrel carb and higher 9.25:1 compression, it was rated at 210 horsepower at 5200 rpm, up 15 bhp and a big jump over the 155-bhp six of 1953-54. Better yet, a special camshaft, cast-aluminum intake manifold, and dual four-barrel carbs increased output to 225-240 bhp. The special cam, developed by Duntov, helped raise torque on the 225-bhp mill to an impressive 270 lbs/ft at 3600 rpm. Powerglide became a $189 option, while the now-standard three-speed manual had closer ratios and worked through a stronger 10-inch clutch. Further, extra-wide 5.5-inch wheels and four-ply high-speed racing tires were newly optional.

Road & Track drove two 225-bhp '56 'Vettes with 3.55:1 gearing and found the going exhilarating: 0-60 in 8.9 and 7.3 seconds (Powerglide/stick shift), 0-100 in 24.0 and 20.7 seconds, the quarter-mile in 16.5 and 15.8 seconds, and a top speed of 121.3 and 129.1 mph. *Sports Car Illustrated* tested the stick with the longer-legged 3.27:1 gearing, doing 0-60 in 7.5 seconds and the quarter-mile in 15.9 seconds at 91 mph. Karl Ludvigsen, *SCI's* test driver, was impressed with the 'Vette in another way: "It is in the handling department that the Corvette proves itself the only true American production sports car."

To prove its mettle, a specially prepared 'Vette (with Duntov cam) went to the Daytona Speed Weeks; in it Duntov managed a two-way run of 150.583 mph. And John Fitch, driving a high-compression 'Vette with about 255 bhp, won the modified class with a two-pass average of 145.543 mph. Then a modified 'Vette placed ninth in the grueling 12-hour race at Sebring, and by the end of the season Dr. Richard Thompson had driven the 'Vette to the SCCA (Sports Car Club of America) C-Production national championship.

But it was at Pebble Beach, California—where Dr. Thompson's 'Vette finished first in class and a strong second overall behind a Mercedes-Benz 300SL—that many say the Corvette emerged as a genuine *first-rank* sports car. And this was only the beginning.

1956 Chevrolet Corvette Major Specifications

Engine:	ohv V-8, 265 cid
	(3.75 × 3.00-in. bore × stroke):
	9.25:1 c.r., 4-bbl carb, 210 bhp;
	9.5:1 c.r., 2 4-bbl carbs, high-lift
	cam, 225-240 bhp
Transmission:	3-speed close-ratio manual;
	2-speed Powerglide opt.
Suspension, front:	unequal-length A-arms,
	coil springs, anti-roll bar
Suspension, rear:	live axle, semi-elliptic
	leaf springs
Brakes:	front/rear drums
Wheelbase (in.):	102.0
Weight (lbs):	2,764
Top speed (mph):	115-129
0-60 mph (sec):	7.3-8.9
Base price:	$3,149
Production:	3,467

Though Chevy didn't promote the Corvette heavily, the few ads that appeared (*above*) told readers to "Get set for a new sight in sports car style and silhouette. Get set for a new sound, a new sensation, a new spirit-lifting surge of the Corvette's dynamic new 225-bhp V8 engine." This was mated to a closer-ratio three-speed Synchro-Mesh shift, with two-speed Powerglide now a $189 option. Chevy also crowed about the new roll-up windows, competition racing steering wheel, side-by-side bucket seats, and "instrumentation as complete as a light plane's." Apparently Chevy was doing something right—production jumped from a lowly 674 units in 1955 to 3467 for '56.

1957 Chevrolet Corvette

By 1957, the Corvette's future looked brighter. Chevrolet managers seemed quite happy to sustain the car despite modest sales and the fact that it was losing money. In fact, there'd been no talk about dropping it since 1955. Appearance didn't change for 1957—it didn't need to—except that the bodyside "coves" could now be finished in a contrasting color.

The important news for 1957 was the new 283 V-8. It has since become one of Chevy's most revered engines—the definitive small-block. It was, of course, the existing 265 engine bored out ⅛-inch (3.875-inch bore × 3.00-inch stroke). In Chevy passenger cars, the 283 delivered 185 bhp in base form, but the standard Corvette version with four-barrel carburetor developed 220 bhp at 4800 rpm. Dual four-barrels took it to 245 and 270 bhp, and GM's newly developed "Ramjet" fuel injection yielded 250 or 283 bhp. The last was the magic "1 h.p. per cu. in.," and Chevy ads blared the news, even

though Chrysler's 300-B had exceeded that ideal in 1956 with its 355-bhp, 354-cid Hemi. The obvious key to higher horsepower was to first enlarge the V-8 and give it better breathing—i.e., more carburetors—both of which were duly done. Chevy then considered supercharging, but deemed the higher internal engine stresses undesirable in terms of reliability. Taking a page from the European performance book, Chevy finally sought more horsepower via more precise fuel metering, which meant fuel injection.

Chevrolet and GM's Rochester carburetor division came up with what we'd now call a mechanical continuous-flow multi-point system with a separate injector for each cylinder, plus a special fuel meter, manifold assembly, and air meter to replace the normal carburetor and intake manifold. The main benefit was increased top-end power spread over a wider rpm band. Alas, reliability problems surfaced quickly, which together with

The '57 Corvette looked just like the '56 model, except that the bodyside "coves" could now be finished in a contrasting color. There was plenty to excite beneath the fiberglass body, however, including a new 283 V-8, four-speed manual shift, Positraction limited-slip differential, and a heavy-duty racing suspension.

the high price—up to $675 for RPO 579E—rendered fuel injection fairly scarce even among Corvettes. Installations ran to 1040 out of total '57 production of 6339 units, about one out of six. Not surprisingly, 713 of them were the hottest performance option: 283-bhp 283 with manual shift (RPO 579B). The others: 579A, 250 bhp/manual, 182 units; 579C, 250 bhp/automatic, 102 units; 579E, 283 bhp/automatic, 43 units.

The four-speed manual gearbox that purists had been demanding was finally announced in May 1957 as a $188 option. It was basically the three-speed Borg-Warner unit with reverse

moved into the tailshaft housing to make room for a fourth forward speed. "Positraction," Chevy's new limited-slip differential, was a separate $45 option. To address complaints about handling and braking deficiencies, Chevrolet issued RPO 684: a $725 "heavy-duty racing suspension" package comprising heavy-duty springs, a thicker front anti-sway bar, Positraction, larger-piston shock absorbers with firmer valving, a faster steering ratio that reduced turns lock-to-lock from 3.7 to 2.9, and ceramic-metallic brake linings with finned ventilated drums. Add the 283-bhp fuelie V-8, and you had a car ready to race right off the showroom floor.

And race it did. At Sebring two production 'Vettes finished 12th and 15th overall and 1-2 in the GT class, the lead car some 20 laps ahead of the nearest Mercedes-Benz 300SL. Back at SCCA, the larger V-8 had bumped the 'Vette into the B-Production class, but it didn't matter as Dr. Richard Thompson took the national championship. But that wasn't all. Corvette took an early season contest down in New Smyrna Beach, Florida, and also swept the first four places at that year's Nassau Speed Weeks and dominated C-Production at Daytona, finishing 1-2-3 in both standing-start acceleration and the flying mile.

In almost any form, the '57 Cor-

This page: The fuel-injected Corvette ran a 283-cubic-inch, 283-horsepower V-8 (with 10.5:1 compression), thus good for "1 h.p. per cu. in." Unfortunately, the Ramjet FI proved troublesome, but all of the 1040 '57 'Vettes that came with it are highly prized collectibles now. One reason, as *Road & Track* put it, was that the 283 fuelie was "an absolute jewel, quiet and remarkably docile when driven gently around town, yet instantly transformable into a roaring brute when pushed hard.... Its best feature is its instantaneous throttle response." *Opposite page*: The '57 Corvette could also be had with dual four-barrel carbs, in which case the horsepower was 245 or 270. Prices this year started at $3465, though this could easily be pushed up another $1000.

vette had absolutely staggering performance. *Motor Trend*'s Walt Woron clocked a 250-bhp fuelie at just 7.2 seconds in the 0-60 sprint. The 283-bhp version was even more incredible. *Road & Track*'s four-speed example with the short 4.11:1 final drive needed only 5.7 seconds 0-60, breezed through the quarter-mile in 14.3 seconds at better than 90 mph, and sailed on to a maximum of 132 mph. An *MT* car with the 283-bhp engine reached 134 mph, and Woron wasn't convinced that it was fully extended at that.

Undoubtedly, 1957 marked the Corvette's arrival as a sports car respected as much by the *cognoscenti* as by the kids on the street. Even a veteran European writer had to admit that "After Sebring, even the most biased were forced to admit that the Americans had one of the world's finest sports cars...."

1957 Chevrolet Corvette Major Specifications

Engine:	ohv V-8, 283 cid
	(3.875 × 3.00-inch bore × stroke):
	9.5:1 c.r., 4-bbl carb, 220 bhp;
	9.5:1 c.r., 2 4-bbl carbs, 245 bhp;
	9.5:1 c.r., high-lift cam, 2 4-bbl
	carbs, 270 bhp; 9.5:1 c.r., FI, 250 bhp;
	10.5:1 c.r., high-lift cam, FI, 283 bhp
Transmission:	3/4 speed manual,
	2-speed Powerglide automatic
Suspension, front:	unequal-length A-arms,
	coil springs, anti-roll bar
Suspension, rear:	live axle, semi-elliptic
	leaf springs
Brakes:	front/rear drums
Wheelbase (in.):	102.0
Weight (lbs):	2,880
Top speed (mph):	115-135
0-60 mph (sec):	5.7-8.0
Base price:	$3,465
Production:	6,339 (1,040 with FI)

1951-52 Chrysler Saratoga Hemi

During the '40s, Chryslers were dependable and well-built. They were also bulky, stodgy-looking cars powered by plodding six- and eight-cylinder L-head engines.

Styling, though smoother up front for '51, remained boxy and upright through 1954, but Chrysler rocked the industry with its engineering prowess in 1951. New were fully hydraulic "Hydraguide" power steering (an industry first) and ventilated brake drums. Even the semi-automatic Fluid Drive transmission was refined into Fluid-Matic, a four-speed with fluid coupling, and Fluid-Torque, which added a torque converter.

What impressed speed freaks, though, was Chrysler's first V-8. Lighter and more efficient than the lazy 135-bhp straight-eight it replaced, the new "FirePower" displaced 331.1 cubic inches, the same as Cadillac's ohv V-8 of 1949. But Chrysler's V-8 boasted hemispherical combustion chambers, which allowed room for the big valves needed for deep breathing and maximum power. Even with relatively low 7.5:1 compression, the FirePower—soon better known as the "Hemi"—belted out 180 horsepower at 4000 rpm and 312 lbs/ft torque at 2000 rpm. Outgunning Cadillac by 20 horses, the Hemi led the '51 horsepower race—and soon became a performance legend.

The Hemi debuted in the big 131.5-inch-wheelbase New Yorkers and Imperials. Then in July 1951, the Hemi appeared in the lower-priced, Windsor-based Saratoga. It handily outran the New Yorker because of its six-inch-shorter length, nimbler 125.5-inch chassis, and 200-250-pound weight advantage—though at 3948 pounds minimum it was no lightweight.

Auto writer Tom McCahill of *Mechanix Illustrated* entered a stock New Yorker in the February 1951 Daytona Beach Speed Weeks, averaging 100.13 mph in the flying mile. He not only copped a class win, but his was the only stock U.S. car to top the century mark. Tommy Thompson drove a New Yorker to victory in a 250-mile NASCAR event in Detroit, demonstrating the Hemi's staying power before envious Motor City executives. And in honor of Chrysler's new-found performance, a New Yorker convertible served as the Official Pace Car for the 1951 Indianapolis 500.

But when it bowed, it was the Saratoga that excited enthusiasts. Driver Bill Sterling contested the 1951 *Carrera Panamericana*, the 2000-plus-mile Mexican Road Race, in a club coupe, winning the stock-car class outright and placing an amazing third overall be-

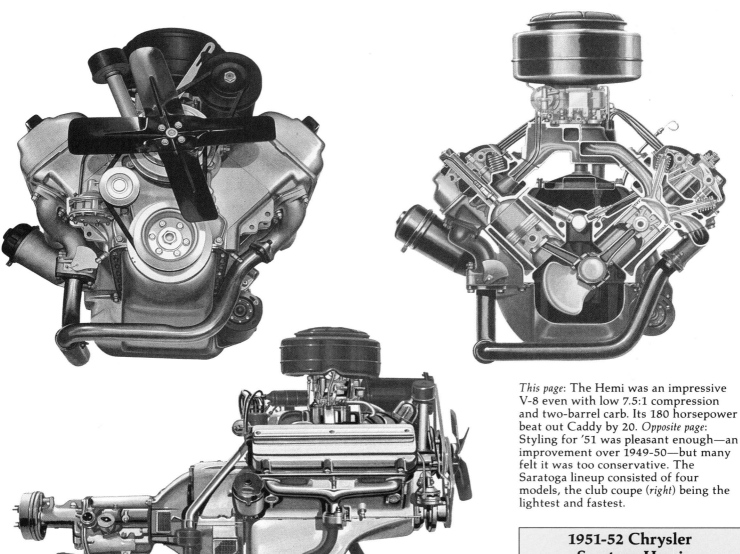

This page: The Hemi was an impressive V-8 even with low 7.5:1 compression and two-barrel carb. Its 180 horsepower beat out Caddy by 20. *Opposite page*: Styling for '51 was pleasant enough—an improvement over 1949-50—but many felt it was too conservative. The Saratoga lineup consisted of four models, the club coupe (*right*) being the lightest and fastest.

hind two Ferraris. In November 1951, *Road & Track* wrung out a Saratoga coupe, and came up with a startling 10.0-second 0-60 dash, this by revving the engine to about 25-percent throttle and "sharply" engaging the clutch. The quarter-mile took 18.7 seconds; top speed was 108.4 mph. *Motor Trend*, treating a '52 sedan more kindly, did 0-60 in 14.8 seconds, 0.4 seconds more than a '51 New Yorker it had tested earlier. Quarter-mile results were also slower, 19.5 seconds versus 19.32, but the Saratoga was faster: 107.6 mph versus 106.1.

MT honored Chrysler with its 1952 Engineering Achievement Award after extensively testing 15 1951 cars. Chrysler—the heavier New Yorker—led or tied in nine of 13 categories. In the 0-60-mph contest no one was even close to Chrysler's 10.63 seconds: Hudson Hornet, 12.52 seconds; Olds Super 88,

13.70; Cadillac Series Sixty-Two, 14.72. In the quarter-mile it was Chrysler in 19.32 seconds, with runners-up Hudson, 19.41; Lincoln, 19.90; and Studebaker, 20.67. Chrysler was also the fastest at 102.27 mph, followed by Hudson, 97.09; Lincoln, 97.08; and Cadillac, 95.44. All cars had automatics, save for the overdrive-equipped Lincoln.

Other than incorporating backup lights into the taillight housings, the '52 Chryslers were reruns, so what was said about the '51 Saratoga also applied to the '52. And incidentally, in 1954 the Hemi was treated to a four-barrel carb and upped to 235 horses, tops in the industry and five up on Cadillac. This helped Brewster Shaw set a new flying-mile record at Daytona at an average speed of 117.065, with Lee Petty right behind at 116.90, both in Chryslers. To top it off, Petty went on to take the NASCAR Grand National

1951-52 Chrysler Saratoga Hemi Major Specifications[1]

Engine:	ohv V-8, 331.1 cid (3.81 × 3.63-in bore × stroke) 7.5:1 c.r., 2-bbl carb, 180 bhp
Transmission:	4-speed semi-automatic Fluid-Matic; 4-speed semi-automatic Fluid-Torque opt.
Suspension, front:	upper and lower A-Arms, coil springs
Suspension, rear:	live axle, semi-elliptic leaf springs
Brakes:	front/rear drums
Wheelbase (in.):	125.5
Weight (lbs):	3,948-4,345
Top speed (mph):	95-108
0-60 mph (sec):	10.0-14.8
Base price:	$2,989-$3,925
Production:	clb cpe 8,501 4d sdn 35,516 Town & Country wgn 1,299 (1951-52 combined)

[1]excluding lwb 8-pass sdn

driving championship that year. Truly, *Road & Track* had it right in 1951 when it observed that "...when you touch that throttle, you know something mighty impressive is happening under the hood."

1955-56 Chrysler 300

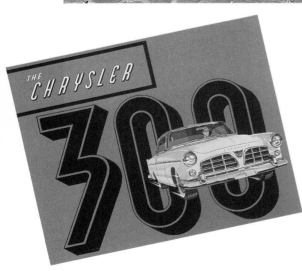

Almost as an afterthought to 1955's "The 100-Million-Dollar Look," Chrysler announced the 300—officially C-300—on February 8, 1955. It was greeted by a cacophony of praise from buff books and stock-car racers and more than a few Chrysler fans who would never even own one. A lot of those who *could* plunk down the $4110 it cost test drove a 300 and bought a New Yorker or Imperial instead. They soon found that what Karl Ludvigsen later called "The Beautiful Brute" was pretty brutish to drive as an everyday car, but that wasn't why it was invented.

There's no doubt that the legendary 300 rates as one of the great performance cars of all time. As *Mechanix Illustrated*'s Tom McCahill put it, it was "the most powerful sedan in the world, and the fastest, teamed up with rock-crushing suspension and a competition engine capable of yanking Bob Fulton's steamboat *over* the George Washington Bridge.... This is definitely not the car for Henrietta Blushbottom, your maiden schoolmarm aunt, to use for hus-

tling up popsicles. In fact, the 300 is not a car for the typical puddling male to use. This is a hardboiled, magnificent piece of semi-competition transportation, built for the real automotive connoisseur."

In fact, a connoisseur conceived the 300: Robert MacGregor Rodger, Chrysler Division's chief engineer and a veteran of the Hemi engine project. It was he who looked at early competition efforts with the Hemi by privateers and decided that the engine deserved factory backing.

Stylist Virgil Exner, who came to dominate Chrysler design with the successful '55s, encouraged Rodger to engineer a super-stock Chrysler, but division general manager Ed Quinn told them both that its styling couldn't deviate too much from the '55 norm. Exner hit upon a combination of Imperial and Chrysler: New Yorker hardtop body; Windsor rear quarter panels; Imperial grille, parking lights, front bumper, and wheel covers. Later, Exner substituted less bulky Chrysler bumpers and parking lights, with Im-

perial bumper guards set far apart. The Imperial dashboard Exner chose sported a 150-mph speedometer, but had no proper space for a tachometer, but this wasn't too serious since the C-300 came only with PowerFlite automatic. Few extras found their way into those first 300s; radio, heater, and power steering were typical. Less often specified were power seats/windows, clock, tinted glass, and wire wheels. Air conditioning wasn't available. Only red, white, and black paint jobs were offered, all combined with tan leather upholstery.

With a hot cam, solid lifters, and two four-barrel carbs, the C-300 boasted 300 horsepower at 5200 rpm and 345 lbs/ft torque at 3200 rpm, making it the most powerful production engine in the world. It proved unbeatable in 1955 competition. It won its first NASCAR (National Association for Stock Car Auto Racing) Grand National at a 92-mph average, and driver Tim Flock was later named NASCAR Grand National Champion for his 18 major wins. The 300 also sped through the Daytona fly-

ing mile at a 127-mph average and set a standing-start mile record for its class at 76.84 mph. Further, Frank Mundy became the AAA Stock Car Champion campaigning a 300. In all, the 300 took the checkered flag at 37 NASCAR and AAA races of more than 100 miles. It underscored Chrysler's already-prominent engineering reputation, sparked sales of more mundane Chryslers, and itself notched up 1725 sales in 1955—good for such a specialized and expensive model.

The finned '56 300-B was a refinement of the '55. Introduced at the Chicago Auto Show in January '56, it featured a Hemi bored out to 354 cid, with 9.0:1 compression, 340 horsepower at 5200 rpm, and 385 lbs/ft torque at 3200 rpm; 355 bhp was optional via 10.0:1 compression heads. It was the first—and last—300 to exceed one horsepower per cubic inch. It also surpassed Packard's 310-bhp Caribbean as the horsepower champion of 1956.

Axle ratios spanned an enormous range, from 3.08:1 to a stump-pulling 6.17:1. No test of the latter is on rec-

The first Chrysler 300, officially C-300, was so named for its horsepower rating. With 331.1 cubic inches, a hot cam, solid lifters, and two four-barrel carbs, it boasted 300 horsepower at 5200 rpm and 345 lbs/ft torque at 3200 rpm, making it the most powerful production engine in the world. Styling (*top row*) was a combination of Imperial and Chrysler: New Yorker hardtop body; Windsor rear quarter panels; plus the Imperial grille, parking lights, front bumper, and wheel covers. The C-300 was bred to race (*above*), and indeed it sped through the Daytona flying mile at a 127-mph average and set a standing-start record for its class at 76.84 mph. The '55 brochure (*far left*) announced the car as simply the Chrysler 300.

The '56 Chrysler 300 received the tailfins and new taillights that were common to all Chryslers that year, but retained its Imperial grille. A "300-B" badge now appeared between the split grilles. A bore job brought displacement up to 354 cubic inches, and horsepower up to 340 on 9.0:1 compression. With a 10.0:1 ratio, horsepower climbed to 355, beating Chevrolet to the magic "1 h.p. per cubic in." by one year. Though more options were available for 1956, such as a "Highway Hi-Fi" record player, the 300 again proved its muscle by dominating at NASCAR.

ord, but it must have done 0-60 in something like four seconds! Again, the 300 dominated NASCAR—Keikhaefer Racing's Tim Flock winning the Grand National race at a 90.836-mph average. At Daytona Beach, the 300-B set an unofficial stock-car record in the flying mile, with a two-way average of 142.914 mph, and Vicki Wood set a new women's world record at 136.081 mph. Flock also broke the world's passenger-car speed record with an official two-way run averaging 139.9 mph. NASCAR was also kind to Buck Baker and his 300—he was named the top driver of the year.

Chrysler offered more options on the 300-B, including factory air and a new RCA "Highway Hi-Fi" record player. But 1956 was a down year sales-wise, so production reached only 1102 units. Be it a '55 or a '56, however, the 300 owner of today is fortunate and widely envied. Notwithstanding the abuses to which the word is subject today, these cars are true classics.

1955-56 Chrysler 300 Major Specifications

Engine:	ohv Hemi V-8
	1955 331.1 cid (3.81 × 3.63-in. bore × stroke), 8.5:1 c.r., 2 4-bbl carbs, solid lifters, 300 bhp **1956** 354 cid (3.94 × 3.63), 9.0:1 c.r., 2 4-bbl carbs, solid lifters, 340 bhp; 10.0:1 c.r., 355 bhp
Transmission:	2-speed PowerFlite automatic 1956 3-speed manual opt.
Suspension, front:	upper and lower A-arms, coil springs
Suspension, rear:	live axle, semi-elliptic leaf springs
Brakes:	front/rear drums
Wheelbase (in.):	126.0
Weight (lbs):	4,005-4,145
Top speed (mph):	110-125
0-60 mph (sec):	9.0-9.8
Base price:	$4,110-$4,419
Production:	**1955 C-300** 1,725 **1956 300-B** 1,102

1957-59 Chrysler 300

With the arrival of Virgil Exner's tailfinned cruisers, torsion-bar front suspension, and three-speed TorqueFlite automatic in 1957, engineer Bob Rodgers and Chrysler Division stayed with their now-established Chrysler 300 formula: an all-out performance car—"semi-competition" as road tester Tom McCahill called it—within the framework of Chrysler production-line components. As the third in the series, the '57 wore a 300-C badge.

The 300-C's distinctive grille was a unique trapezoidal affair flanked by either dual or quad headlights, the latter not yet legal everywhere. Below them were small intakes that channeled air directly to enlarged front brake drums. This was the year of the flying MoPar tailfins, all of them elegantly done, but Chrysler's were particularly well integrated with the dart-shaped lines of the car.

Mechanical refinements to the 300-C included a larger 392-cid V-8 with

Styling was all-new across the board at Chrysler Corporation for 1957. In addition, the 300, now badged 300-C, sported its own unique, and aggressive-looking, grille. Adding to the flavor were air ducts for brake cooling located just below the newly allowed (in most states) quad headlights. Base price for the ragtop, new to the line, was $5359.

SilentFlow fan drive, which boosted power by automatically stopping the radiator fan at 2500 rpm. The 300's torsion bars were 40 percent stiffer than those of the New Yorker, so it rode as hard as ever. Power steering cost extra, but proved useful since it required only 3.3 turns lock-to-lock; most 300-Cs had it.

Like the Windsor, the 300 could be ordered with a three-speed manual shift, part of an Optional Chassis Package. In lieu of the 375-bhp, 420-lbs/ft-torque standard V-8, the package consisted of a longer-duration cam and 10.0:1 compression, upping horse-

1957-59 Chrysler 300-E Major Specifications

Engine:	ohv V-8, 392 cid (4.00 × 3.90-in. bore × stroke)
	1957 9.25:1 c.r., 2 4-bbl carbs, 375 bhp; 10.0:1 c.r., 390 bhp opt. **1958** 10.0:1 c.r., 2 4-bbl carbs, 380 bhp; FI, 390 bhp opt. **1959** 413 cid (4.18 × 3.75), 10.0:1 c.r., 2 4-bbl carbs, 380 bhp
Transmission:	3-speed manual; 3-speed TorqueFlite automatic
Suspension, front:	upper and lower control arms, longitudinal torsion bars, anti-roll bar
Suspension, rear:	live axle, semi-elliptic leaf springs
Brakes:	front/rear drums
Wheelbase (in.):	126.0
Weight (lbs):	4,235-4,475
Top speed (mph):	110-120
0-60 mph (sec):	7.7-9.1
Base price:	$4,235-$5,749
Production:	1957 300-C htp cpe 1,918
	cvt 484 1958 300-D htp cpe 618
	cvt 191 1959 300-E htp cpe 550
	cvt 140

power to a whopping 390, plus low-pressure exhaust and manual steering. Chrysler advised that the package "is not recommended for the average 300-C customer" because of the lumpy idle and poorer low-speed performance.

New to the 300 series was a convertible, representing about a third of production. As with past 300s, however, 300-C trim options remained limited: tan leather again for all interiors, with a choice of just five exterior colors.

Readers of Tom McCahill's road tests in *Mechanix Illustrated* knew that the Chrysler 300 was right up his alley. He described the '57 as "the most hairy-chested, fire-eating land bomb ever conceived in Detroit." He reported 0-60 mph in 8.4 seconds with TorqueFlite, and a top speed of 150 with a high (low numerical) rear axle

ratio. Unfortunately, the 300's dominance of racing was ending because the Auto Manufacturers Association instituted a ban on racing promotion. But that didn't stop the 300-C from taking the standing- and flying-mile championships at Daytona, with privateer Brewster Shaw exceeding 130 mph in the latter.

Changes were slight on the 300-D: a simpler eggcrate grille and smaller taillights. A standard 10.0:1 compression ratio upped horsepower to 380 at 5200 rpm and torque to 435 lbs/ft at 3600 rpm. Bendix Electrojector fuel injection, a $400 option, provided 390 bhp (but no more torque). Ordered on only 16 cars, it proved unreliable, so most were converted to dual four-barrel carbs. Power brakes came standard, though manual shift meant manual

steering and brakes along with no air. In one of its few competitive outings, the 300-D set a new speed record: 156.387 mph in Class E at Bonneville, with Norm Thatcher driving. Brewster Shaw showed up again at Daytona, turning a quarter-mile in 16 seconds at 94 mph. There was no doubt that the 1958 300-D was still a brute.

The '59 300-E retained its distinctive trapezoidal grille and clean flanks bearing the traditional 300 emblem and spear, but wore 1959-style taillights, rear bumper, and deck. These didn't help styling, and worse, a rumor surfaced that the 300 had lost its fangs. Reason? The Hemi had given way to a wedge-head V-8. Not only that, it had hydraulic lifters. On the other hand, it had more cubes—413 of them—plus it was 101 pounds lighter and had a high-

Opposite page: The 300-C (*top*) took the standing- and flying-mile championships at Daytona in 1957. Only 484 buyers drove a 300-C convertible (*bottom*) home. *This page*: The '58 300-D, here the $5173 hardtop (*left*), boasted 380 horses, 390 with the rarely installed fuel injection. For the 300-E (*below*), '59-style Chrysler trim graced the rear end, and the Hemi was replaced by a 413-cid wedge-head V-8 rated at 380 horsepower. Sales skidded to 140 convertibles and 550 hardtops. Where's the tach (*bottom*)?

output cam, though not as "wild" as before. The result was 380 horses at 5000 rpm and 450 lbs/ft torque at 3600 rpm.

Given the racing ban, Chrysler touted the 300-E as a luxury-performance car, so a full range of New Yorker-like equipment joined the options list. Included were swivel seats, Auto Pilot cruise control, and a "toilet seat" fake spare tire cover on the rear deck. Leather still swathed the interior, but the fluff and non-functional ephemera such as unventilated wheel covers with phoney hubs made some people wonder if the 300-E had become a paper tiger. It hadn't.

Take, for example, a March 1959 *Motor Trend* report: "Performance of the 300E tops its predecessor by a good margin. The 300E this year weighs a little over 4300 pounds at the curb. The big

380-bhp engine (with 10.0:1 compression, improved TorqueFlite transmission, and 3.31 to 1 rear end) handles this poundage with no difficulty at all." Chrysler's own engineering figures virtually duplicated *MT*'s data. Both showed the 300-E doing 0-60 in a little over eight seconds, and Chrysler reported a 0-90-mph blast in 17.6 seconds versus 20.6 seconds for the 300-D.

Unfortunately, the mixed message Chrysler was sending about this new 300 turned off traditional customers while failing to attract luxury buyers, who chose a New Yorker instead. Money was a factor, too, for the New Yorker cost $900 less than the 300-E. In a year of improving sales, the "E" had the lowest production to date.

The song had ended, it seemed, but the memory lingers on.

1956 DeSoto Adventurer

The impact of the Chrysler 300 on sales of more ordinary "civilian" Chryslers was not lost on the Highland Park corporation. It was a relatively simple business to apply the same kind of factory hot-rodding to other makes in the Chrysler stable, producing a limited-edition performance model for each Chrysler division. This occurred in 1956, when Plymouth announced the Fury, Dodge the D-500 performance package, and DeSoto wheeled out the $3728 Adventurer hardtop—one of the highest-priced DeSotos ever. Few were built, but this wildly decorated, mighty road machine brought many a soul into DeSoto-Plymouth showrooms, to emerge clutching an order slip for more mundane models.

The Adventurer name had been coined by Virgil Exner in 1954 for one of his Ghia-bodied show cars built in Turin to his specifications, using DeSoto componentry. Cast in the image of the K-310, the '51 show car that had helped transform Chrysler's stodgy image, the compact Adventurer measured only 190 inches long and rode a 111-inch, shortened DeSoto chassis. It was by far the smallest Exner showmobile—the K-10 stretched out over two feet longer. Since most of its length rested between the wheels, the Adventurer could accommodate four passengers comfortably. Painted off-white, the handsome coupe sported a black leather interior, full instrumentation and, of course, the 276.1-cid DeSoto Hemi V-8. "It was my favorite," Exner said later. "I owned it for three years and kept it at home."

Later the same year, Ghia built the

DeSoto's first limited-edition, high-performance model was the '56 Adventurer. It could easily by told from lesser models because of its eggshell white paint job, gold roof and sweepspear, and gold-spoked wheel covers.

Adventurer II, which lacked bumpers, giving it what stylists joked was a toothless "Andy Gump" appearance at the front end. Designed almost wholly by Ghia, the Adventurer II's most novel feature was a retracting rear window that slid into the trunk, following the rakish lines of the sleek roof. Despite a standard wheelbase, its styling handled the length well, with graceful rounded lines.

DeSoto announced the production Adventurer in time for the spring selling season, and the entire production run of 996 units was sold out within

six weeks of introduction. There was no mistaking the few that were built, with their eggshell white paint job, contrasting gold roof and sweepspear, and special anodized gold, pseudo-spoked

wheel covers. A similarly trimmed Pacesetter convertible with a tuned 255-bhp Fireflite V-8, introduced a month earlier, had paced the Indianapolis 500. But what most distinguished the Adventurer lurked under the hood, and that's what paced the '56 Pikes Peak hill climb.

DeSoto still offered its three-speed manual gearbox on the '56 Firedome, but this was not a performance transmission. Thus, the Adventurer, like the Fireflite, came with standard PowerFlite two-speed automatic. The engine, a slightly bored out version of the '56 Hemi with a ¾-race camshaft, produced 320 horsepower: 65 more than the Fireflite, 90 more than the Firedome. Following the formula of the other Chrysler performance specials, the Adventurer received stiffer-

than-stock springs and shocks, producing a taut ride—not every DeSoto customer's cup of tea. But it certainly resulted in excellent handling for so heavy a car—the Adventurer weighed only 100 pounds less than the Chrysler 300-B and measured just two inches shorter overall.

Test driver Don MacDonald borrowed the last Adventurer not already in private hands, a brand new car that had not been broken in. At Daytona Beach, he flew through the clocks on the sand at 137 mph, but the same car later did 144 around the Chrysler proving ground track at Chelsea, Michigan. Surprisingly, the Adventurer was only marginally quicker than the '56 Fireflite, but MacDonald attributed this to the car's newness: "The small difference in low-speed acceleration be-

The dual exhausts hint that the '56 Adventurer (*below*) ran with a 341.4-cid Hemi V-8 that cranked out 320 bhp. Don MacDonald drove an Adventurer that hadn't even been broken in to 137 mph at Daytona. The Pacesetter convertible, an Indy 500 Pace Car replica, featured an interior (*left*) nearly identical with the Adventurer.

tween the '56 Fireflite and the Adventurer is attributable to the ¾-race cam which favors high-end performance. Actually, give or take the spread between production cars of the same make, a '56 Fireflite will get ahead of an Adventurer between 0-40 mph, but don't carry the same race on up to 90 mph or you will lose." The figures are revealing:

	'55 Fireflite[1]	'56 Fireflite	'56 Adventurer
bhp	200	255	320
0-30 mph	4.3 sec	4.0 sec	4.0 sec
0-60 mph	12.1 sec	10.9 sec	10.5 sec
¼-mile	18.9, 77 mph	17.8, 78.5 mph	17.5, 81 mph
35-50 mph	4.7 sec	3.9 sec	3.9 sec
50-80 mph	13.2 sec	11.2 sec	10.4 sec
Top speed	118 mph	108.7 mph	144 mph

[1]Manual transmission, "Hi-Tork" differential

Driving the Adventurer was obviously an adventure. Like the Chrysler 300, it was too much car for the average driver, but proved how fast and agile a big Detroiter could be.

1957-59 DeSoto Adventurer

Many people have fond memories of 1957. A lot happened that year. The Everly Brothers went to the top of the record charts with "Bye, Bye Love." In January, President Eisenhower took the oath of office for his second term, promising to erase the government's shocking $4 billion budget deficit. Appearing in bookstores was Jack Kerouac's semi-autobiographical novel *On The Road*, which introduced a new word to America: beatnik. Chrysler Corporation was also making introductions that year: "Torsion-Aire" ride, three speed TorqueFlite automatic, more powerful engines, and "Flite Sweep" styling, the latest expression of "The Forward Look."

All Chrysler Corporation cars were completely restyled for 1957, and one could argue that the DeSoto was the best looking of the lot. The two upper series, Firedome and Fireflite, wore a broad bumper/grille, with a full-width oval jutting out above a rectangular mesh panel. Headlamps were sunk into nacelles sized to accept either the usual two-lamp system or the new "four-eyes" arrangement newly legal in most states. The lower-priced Firesweep used the same grille, but achieved a different look with heavily eyebrowed headlamps from the '57 Dodge. All DeSotos continued with vertically stacked triple taillights, and oval dual exhaust outlets protruded di-

The '57 DeSoto Adventurer had a lot going for it: torsion-bar front suspension, slick-shifting TorqueFlite automatic, all-new styling. And there was power: 345 horses from 345 cubes.

rectly below, forming a "base" for the soaring fins. Bodyside contrast color panels were shaped roughly the same as in '56.

The Firesweeps used a wedge-head 361-cid V-8 offering 245 and 260 horsepower, while the more expensive models boasted a 341-cid Hemi rated at 270 and 290 bhp. Two months after the debut of the '57s, DeSoto trotted out the Adventurer, a high-priced, high-

45

performance car similar in concept to the '56. This time, however, there were two models: a $3997 hardtop and, even later in the model run, a $4272 convertible.

As in 1956, Adventurers were identified by exterior gold trim and rear fender nameplates, plus deluxe interiors. The standard equipment list was long, and it included the new pushbutton TorqueFlite three-speed automatic transmission.

Backing up the Adventurer's dashing good looks was a firm suspension and a 345-cubic-inch Hemi V-8. Running with 9.25:1 compression and dual four-barrel carbs, it developed 345 horsepower—giving it the same magic "1 h.p. per cubic inch" that Chevy was shouting about this year for its fuel injected 283-cid V-8. It should be noted, however, that DeSoto was the first U.S. make to offer that one-bhp per cubic inch as *standard*—the 283-bhp Chevy V-8 and the 355-bhp, 354-cid '56 Chrysler 300-B engines were optional, and rarely installed. And even at a hefty 4040 pounds for the hardtop, the Adventurer was about 200 pounds lighter than the '57 300-C, canceling out much of the Chrysler's 30 horsepower advantage. Not only that, the DeSoto was $900 cheaper.

As in 1956, the Adventurer was extremely quick. Fast-shifting Torque-

Flite and the torsion-bar front suspension made it among the most roadworthy cars as well. A Firedome with the Turboflash V-8 and the optional 305-bhp setup could accelerate from 0-60 in 7.7 seconds, to 80 mph in 13.5 seconds, and could reach 115 mph with little strain. The Adventurer was even quicker, good for up to 125 mph.

The '58 Adventurer, introduced in January 1958 at the Chicago Auto

Show, sported a mild—and not entirely successful—facelift. The most obvious change was the bodyside trim, which on Adventurers featured triangular inserts (with nameplate) on the rear fenders. Gold highlights were present again, and the decklid sported chrome rub strips. More significantly, the Hemi was gone, replaced by a 361-cid wedge-head engine that developed the same 345 horsepower with twin

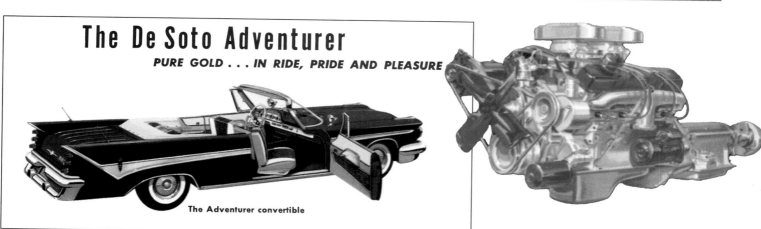

The De Soto Adventurer
PURE GOLD . . . IN RIDE, PRIDE AND PLEASURE

The Adventurer convertible

1957-59 DeSoto Adventurer Major Specifications

Engine:	ohv V-8 **1957** 345 cid (3.80 × 3.80-in. bore × stroke), 9.25:1 c.r., 2 4-bbl carbs, 345 bhp **1958** 361 cid (4.125 × 3.375), 10.25:1 c.r., 2 4-bbl carbs, 345 bhp; FI, 355 bhp opt. **1959** 383 cid (4.25 × 3.375), 10.0:1 c.r., 2 4-bbl carbs, 350 bhp
Transmission:	3-speed TorqueFlite automatic
Suspension, front:	independent, torsion bars, tube shocks
Suspension, rear:	live axle, leaf springs, tube shocks (rear air suspension opt. 1959, $140)
Brakes:	front/rear drums
Wheelbase (in.):	126.0
Weight (lbs):	4,040-4,235
Top speed (mph):	120-125
0-60 mph (sec):	7.0-9.0
Base price:	$3,997-$4,749
Production:	**1957** htp cpe 1,650 cvt 300 **1958** htp cpe 350 cvt 82 **1959** htp cpe 590 cvt 97

quads as the '57. With optional—and expensive ($637.20)—Bendix electronic fuel injection, horsepower rose to 355 at 5000 rpm, making this the mightiest car DeSoto would ever build. Unfortunately, the fuel injection, noted with front-fender badges, proved so troublesome that the few cars so equipped were recalled to be retro-fitted with carburetors.

The '59 DeSotos received an extensive facelift marked by a heavy-looking gold-trimmed grille and revised side trim. Adventurers strutted bodyside gold anodized aluminum inserts, front-fender nameplates, rear-fender medallions, chrome strips on the decklid, and textured paint on the hardtop's roof for a leather-grain look. As before, twin four-barrel carbs were used, this time on a 383-cubic-inch mill with 10.0:1 compression and high-lift cams. It cranked out 350 horsepower at 5000 rpm and was available at $108-$142 on

Opposite page: The '59 Adventurer boasted updated styling and 350 horses from 383 cubes. Both engines ran with dual four-barrels, but the '57 was a Hemi, the '59 a wedge-head. *This page*: The gold trim on the '59 Adventurer (*top*) really stood out against a black paint job. DeSoto called it "Pure gold...in ride, pride and pleasure." The decklid trim was optional on other DeSotos. Inside the Fashion-Vogue Interior, Sports Swivel Seats eased entry (*center*). DeSoto credited the engine with smooth response and "split-second precision" to the TorqueFlite gearbox.

other models. Likewise, the decklid ribs could be had on lesser DeSotos for a mere $11. Alas, the '59s would be the last true high-performance Adventurers. Just two years later, after building 2,024,629 cars—only 4065 of them 1956-59 Adventurers—DeSoto would itself become history, but the ultimate DeSotos left a fine legacy for a make that deserved to live.

47

1953-54 Dodge V-8

Chevrolet's mid-'50s transformation from dull to dynamite is well known, but it's often forgotten that Dodge underwent a similar metamorphosis two years before. The year was 1953 and it was largely accomplished with the fabled Hemi V-8. Named for its "half-a-dome" combustion-chamber shape, the Hemi had set Detroit performance on its ear when introduced on the 1951 Chrysler, and a year later on DeSoto.

Though costlier to build, the Hemi offered a number of advantages over conventional V-8s with wedge-shape combustion chambers. Chief among them was that the spark plug could be positioned in the center of the chamber, rather than off to one side, for more complete combustion and higher thermal efficiency. This allowed larger valves spaced farther apart, which meant faster, fuller cylinder "filling" of the air/fuel mixture. Other pluses were smoother porting and manifolding, larger water passages for superior cooling, and less heat loss to coolant,

permitting a smaller, lighter radiator. It all added up to an engine packing more punch per cubic inch.

Punch was something Dodge definitely needed by 1953. Though ever admired for rugged dependability—but little else—a falling sales curve suggested a change was needed yesterday. Company planners thus put the rush on flashy all-new '55 designs, and did what they could to give the 1953-54 models more pizzazz. In the end, the '53s were a compromise: more stylish than the 1949-52 "boxes," but smaller and still primly upright next to most rivals. Aided by its "vest-pocket" Hemi, Dodge scored higher 1953 volume, partly because the government had lifted Korean War restrictions on production. But in 1954, facing flashy all-new Buicks and Oldsmobiles, Dodge sales plunged by more than half, dropping it to eighth in industry standings.

Still, the '53 was a big step in the right direction. Dubbed "Red Ram," the Hemi arrived with 241.3 cubic inches and 140 horsepower at 4400 rpm

(220 lbs/ft torque at 2000 rpm) for a new Coronet Eight series on 114- and 119-inch wheelbases. In addition to the neat and trim styling, Dodge also boasted a new double-channel "Road Action" chassis with revised front suspension. Transmissions included a pair of semi-automatic options: Gyrol Fluid Drive and Gyro-Torque, the latter with torque converter.

Tom McCahill wrote in *Mechanix Illustrated* that the Red Ram V-8 "all but straightens out the horns on that hood-ornament goat when you jump the accelerator." With Gyro-Torque, he covered the 0-60 run in 15.11 seconds and estimated that with stick/overdrive he could have bettered that by two seconds. Top speed was just over 100 mph. In 1954, "Uncle" Tom did 0-60 in 14.2 seconds with the 150-bhp Red Ram (standard in Coronet V-8s and Royals) mated to the new PowerFlite two-speed automatic.

Changes for 40th Anniversary 1954 embraced detail styling changes and an expanded lineup headed by a quartet of

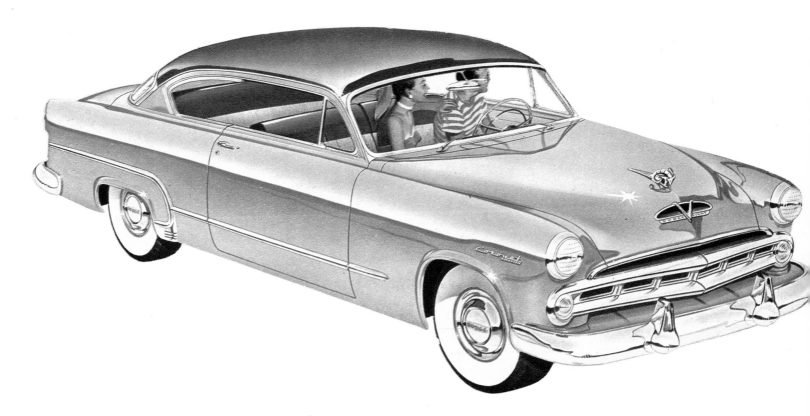

The '53 Dodge Coronet Diplomat (*opposite*) proudly announced its new Hemi V-8 via a "V" badge centered on a functional hood air scoop. Dodge advertised itself (*right*) as "The Action Car For Active Americans." Ads often featured the 241.3-cid, 140-bhp Hemi, and PR eagerly passed out photos and negatives of it to the press (*below*). The '54 Dodge sported a new grille and bodyside chrome, the car here (*bottom*) being a rare specially trimmed Royal for the spring selling season.

posh Royal V-8s. A fifth Royal arrived at mid-season: the hot 500 convertible, a replica of the Dodge Indy 500 Official Pace Car. Featured were a tuned Hemi, Kelsey-Hayes chrome wire wheels, "continental" spare tire, and special ornamentation. Dodge also offered the pace car's power in lesser Dodges via a dealer-installed Offenhauser manifold with four-barrel carburetor; output wasn't revealed, but estimates placed it around 200 horses.

Dodge sold only a handful of Royal 500s, but the Red Ram had already shown its prowess. Danny Eames drove a '53 to a record 102.6 mph at El Mirage dry lake in California, and Dodge was victorious in a half-dozen NASCAR events. In September 1953, a factory team set 196 new AAA stock-car speed records at Bonneville, including 53 endurance marks and the flying 10-mile at 108.36 mph. Just as impressive, Dodge V-8s finished 1-2-3-4-6-9 in the Medium Stock class at the '54 running of the gruelling *Carrera Panamericana*.

With all this, Dodge had become a performance power to be reckoned with.

1953-54 Dodge V-8 Major Specifications

Engine: ohv V-8, 241.3 cid (3.44 × 3.25-in. bore × stroke) **1953-54** 7.1:1 c.r., 2-bbl Stromberg carb, 140 bhp **1954** 7.5:1 c.r., 150 bhp; Performance pkg with dealer-installed Offenhauser manifold and 4-bbl carb, 200 bhp est., opt.

Transmission: 3-speed manual; overdrive, 4-speed Gyrol Fluid Drive/Gyro-Torque semi-automatics opt. **1954** 2-speed PowerFlite automatic opt.

Suspension, front: upper and lower A-arms, coil springs, anti-roll bar

Suspension, rear: live axle, semi-elliptic leaf springs

Brakes: front/rear drums

Wheelbase (in.): 114.0/119.0

Weight (lbs): 3,325-3,660

Top speed (mph): 95-110; Performance pkg, 120 est.

0-60 mph (sec): 13.0-15.5; Performance pkg, 10.0 est.

Production: **1953 Coronet Eight club cpe** 32,439 **4d sdn** 24,059 **cvt** 4,100 **Diplomat 2d htp** 17,334 **Sierra 2d wgn** 5,400 **1954 Coronet V-8 club cpe** 7,998 **4d sdn** 36,063 **Sport 2d htp** 100 **cvt** 50 **Suburban 2d wgn** 3,100 **Sierra 4d wgn** 988 **Royal V-8 club cpe** 8,900 **4d sdn** 50,050 **Sport 2d htp** 3,852 **cvt** 2,000 (incl. 701 Royal 500s) **chassis** 1

1956-59 Dodge D-500

Dodge's traditional conservative look was blown away for good by all-new sheetmetal and flashy two- and three-toning for 1955. The wheelbase rose to 120 inches across the board, overall length to 212.1. Meanwhile, a bore expansion gave the Red Ram V-8 270.1-cubic inches and 175 bhp; the Super Red Ram was good for 183/193 horses.

Modest "Jet-Fin" tailfins sprouted on the otherwise similar-looking '56 Dodge, which boasted a Red Ram V-8 stroked to 315 cubes. Horsepower was 189, but Super Red Rams offered 218 bhp with 8.0:1 compression, 230 with a four-barrel carb. Then, early in the calendar year, the D-500 option blasted onto the scene. Chrysler was into specific high-performance models now with the Plymouth Fury, DeSoto Adventurer, and Chrysler 300-B, but there was no such offering at Dodge. Instead, D-500 power could be had on *any* model, right down to the lightest, cheapest Coronet two-door sedan. Or even on the chauvinistic La Femme

While the other Chrysler Corporation makes each had a specific high-performance model for 1956, Dodge chose instead a D-500 engine package available on any model, such as the Royal Lancer hardtop (*opposite*). *This page*: Dodge's '56 ads bragged about records set at the Bonneville Salt Flats (*top left*) and told readers that the D-500 was a real bomb (*top right*). The '57 Dodge was all-new, and the decklid badge on this Coronet soft top (*center and bottom*) announced that it was a D-500.

which, for "Her Royal Majesty," came in a pink and white paint job (two-tone lavender for 1956) with gold-fleck upholstery and special compartments for milady's cosmetics, umbrella, etc. Only about 1000 were built in 1955-56.

An even rarer trim option was the mid-1956 Golden Lancer, a companion to the Plymouth Fury painted gold and white, with gold-accented interior hardware and special upholstery. A striking looker, it was also impressive at traffic lights because of its standard D-500 engine.

Actually, there were two D-500 V-8s: one with 9.25:1 compression, Carter four-barrel carb, and 260 bhp; the other with twin four-barrels and a rubber-burning 295 horses. In one road test, the 260-bhp D-500 Royal Lancer two-door hardtop dashed from 0-60 mph in just 8.8 seconds.

With that kind of power, 1956 was one of Dodge's best years in racing. For example, a '56 D-500 shattered every U.S. closed car speed record at Bonneville in late 1955. Further, Dodge ranked third—ahead of every make in its class—in NASCAR manufacturer point standings. Though the Chrysler 300 won 22 Grand National events against Dodge's 10, Chrysler piled up only 431 manufacturer's points compared to Dodge's 536. The best performance of the year was a 1-2-3 win at the Virginia 500. Alas, Petty Engineering switched to Oldsmobile for 1957 and Carl Kiekhaefer, whose sponsorship had been crucial in 1956, dropped out of racing, so Dodge would be out of the NASCAR running until the return of the Hemi in 1964.

The drastically new "Swept-Wing" 1957 Dodges were lower, wider, chromier, and more colorful—faster and flashier than ever before. The Red Ram Hemi got 10 more cubes for a total of 325; in D-500 trim, with 10.0:1 compression, single four-barrel carb,

D-500 choices for the '57 Dodge Custom Royal Lancer hardtop (*top*) were 285 bhp with a four-barrel carb and 310 and 340 bhp with dual four-barrels, the first two with the 325-cid Hemi, the last with a 354 Hemi. For 1958 (*bottom*), styling changed only in detail, but the top engine was now a 361-cid wedge with a four-barrel and 305 bhp, twin-quads and 320 bhp, or the rare fuel injection and 333 horses.

1956-59 Dodge D-500 Major Specifications

Engine:	ohv V-8 **1956** 315 cid (3.63 × 3.80-in. bore × stroke), 9.25:1 c.r., 4-bbl carb, 260 bhp; 2 4-bbl-carbs, 295 bhp **1957** 325 cid (3.69 × 3.80), 10.0:1 c.r., 4-bbl carb, 285 bhp; 2 4-bbl carbs, 310 bhp; 354 cid (3.94 × 3.63), 340 bhp **1958** 361 cid (4.12 × 3.38), 10.0:1 c.r., 4-bbl carb, 320 bhp; FI, 333 bhp **1959** 383 cid (4.25 × 3.38), 10.1:1 c.r., 4-bbl carb, 320 bhp; 2 4-bbl carbs, 345 bhp
Transmission:	3-speed manual; overdrive, 2-speed PowerFlite, 3-speed Torque-Flite opt.
Suspension, front:	upper and lower A-arms, coil springs, anti-roll bar (1957-59)
Suspension, rear:	live axle, semi-elliptic leaf springs
Brakes:	front/rear drums
Wheelbase (in.):	**1956** 120.0 **1957-59** 122.0
Weight (lbs):	3,380-4,020
Top speed (mph):	105-115
0-60 mph (sec):	8.8-9.8
Base price:	$2,302-$3,439
Production (all models):	**1956** 240,686 **1957** 287,608 **1958** 137,861 **1959** 156,385 (D-500 option available on all models each year; no separate installation breakdown available)

and solid lifters, it put out 285 bhp. There was again a dual-quad Super D-500, and it was super with 310 horses. A very few 1957s even had the 354-cid, 340-horse engine from the Chrysler 300-B, and carried a D-501 label.

The '57s were doubly blessed with front "Torsion-Aire" suspension, making them among the best handlers on the road, and three-speed TorqueFlite automatic, so good that even drag racers favored it. D-500s also came with stiffened shocks, torsion bars, and rear leaf springs for what one magazine termed "close liaison with the road." Even the typical base V-8 could do 0-60 in around 10 seconds; a D-500 Custom Royal sedan was timed by one maga-

zine at 9.4 seconds. Super D-500s could cut that to about eight seconds.

Trim was shuffled for 1958—and the Hemi was shuffled off the engine list by Chrysler's new wedge-head V-8. For the D-500 this meant 361 cubic inches, 10.0:1 compression, hydraulic lifters, four-barrel carb, and 305 bhp. Super D-500s added either Carter twin four-barrels for 320 bhp at 4600 rpm or Bendix electronic fuel injection for 333 bhp at 4800 rpm. The latter was a reliability disaster, so the dozen or so units installed were recalled to be exchanged for carburetors. In defense of the wedge-head, a 320-bhp Super D-500 in a heavy Lancer four-door hardtop body zipped from 0-60 in 9.3

seconds, according to one test report.

While several makes cut their performance options for 1959, Dodge didn't. Engine sizes and power outputs went up, so civilians would have been able to give police cars a theoretical run for it. The D-500 and Super D-500, now based on the wedge-head 383, pumped out 320 bhp at 4600 rpm with 10.1:1 compression and a four-barrel carb and 345 bhp at 5000 rpm with twin four-pots. Racing appearances were sparse now, but on the road Dodge rarely took a back seat to anyone in the performance and handling departments. And Dodge would be back with a vengeance with a mighty 426 Hemi in the Sixties!

1955-56 Ford V-8

Under Henry II, Ford Motor Company underwent a renaissance following World War II. Having surpassed Chrysler Corporation by 1952, Henry began an assault on GM in 1953. By loading dealers with cars that had to be sold at deep discounts, and helped by the lure of its new overhead-valve V-8, Ford came within 23,000 units of unseating Chevrolet in 1954.

It might seem surprising, then, that the '55 Ford wasn't as completely new-from-the-ground-up as was the '55 Chevy. No matter—Chevy was playing catch-up, for Ford had introduced that new V-8 and ball-joint suspension in 1954, and had provided features such as suspended brake and clutch pedals as far back as 1952.

Ford's 1955 offensive emphasized style and performance. Design-wise, the heavily reworked Ford sported a wraparound windshield, stylish two-toning, hooded headlamps, concave grille, rear fenders hinting at fins, and big, round taillights. There was also a flashy new Fairlane Crown Victoria

with a distinctive "basket handle" roof treatment, available with or without a transparent roof over the front seat.

In 1954, Ford had stolen a lead on Chevrolet (and Plymouth) with the first modern V-8 in the low-price field, a smooth, efficient "Y-Block" sized at 239.4 cubic inches. The '55 "Trigger-Torque" version was bored and stroked to 272 cid; with a Holley two-barrel

The '55 Fairlane was the brashest, splashiest Ford ever, and with the 182-horsepower version of the 272 V-8 it could step out quite smartly as well. New-for-'55 design features included a full-width concave eggcrate grille, wraparound windshield, heavily browed headlights, fancy two-toning, and large round taillights. The $2224 Sunliner convertible found 49,966 buyers.

carb and 7.6:1 compression, it churned out 162 horsepower at 4400 rpm, up from 130. A "Power Pack"—8.5:1 compression, four-barrel carb, and dual exhausts—lifted that to 182 bhp and boosted torque from 258 lbs/ft at 2200 rpm to 268. Aside from the 120-bhp six, there were two other options. One was a bigger-bore 292 V-8 with 8.5:1 compression, four-barrel carb, 198 horses, and Fordomatic, a special-order package for Fairlanes and wagons. Late in the year, a 205-bhp "Interceptor" 292, ostensibly for police use, appeared as an outgrowth of the factory's efforts in NASCAR stock-car racing.

Ford's 1951-vintage slushbox gained a new kickdown feature for 1955,

which with the added horsepower shaved up to three seconds off 0-60-mph trips. Flooring the throttle provided an automatic downchange into Low (manually selected with earlier Fordomatics, which started in Second). The standard transmission remained the three-speed column-shift manual, with overdrive optional. Further, brakes were larger and the ball-joint suspension was tilted slightly rearward to absorb road shocks from the front as well as vertically. That suspension had moved *Motor Trend* to call the '54 Ford America's most roadable car.

The typical Fordomatic-equipped 272 could do 0-60 in 14 seconds and reach a shade over 100 mph. The Power Pack

shaved 1.0-1.5 seconds off the 0-60 time.

Though Ford emphasized safety in its mildly facelifted '56s, performance wasn't forgotten. A compression increase to 8.0:1 gave the six a 17-bhp jump to 137, while the 272 gained 11 horses for 173/176 in all. The Power Pack option was scratched, but the four-barrel 292 with duals was rated at 200 bhp, 202 with Fordomatic. Topping the chart was a hot new Y-block, the 312-cid "Thunderbird Special," offering 215/225 bhp (manual/automatic). This promised high excitement in a light Tudor sedan—any engine was available in any model. A 245-bhp twin four-barrel version arrived at mid-year as a T-Bird option, and a few

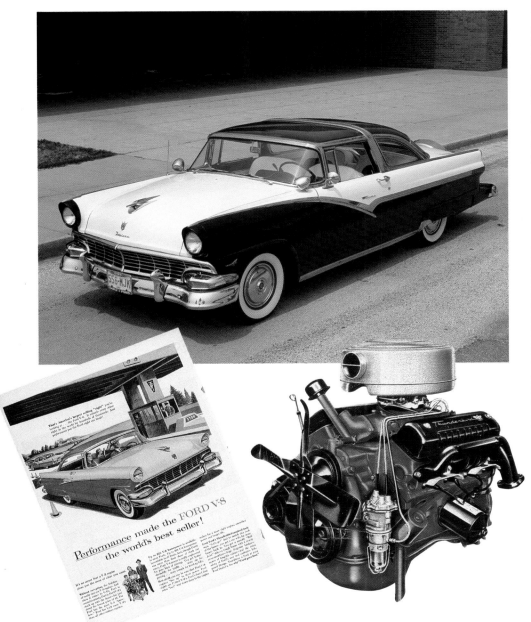

The '56 Ford strutted a modest—and attractive—facelift, centering mainly on the grille and side trim. Model offerings encompassed the $2249 Fairlane Victoria sedan (*opposite, top*), $1939 Customline Tudor (*opposite, bottom*), and $2337 Fairlane Crown Victoria (*left*). Note the "Thunderbird Y-8" emblems on the front fenders, and the engine itself (*below*). One ad (*below left*) said "You get better skedaddle in traffic... more zip for passing... more oomph for leveling hills."

Performance made the FORD V-8 the world's best seller!

1955-56 Ford V-8 Major Specifications	
Engine:	ohv V-8 **1955** 272 cid (3.62 × 3.30-in. bore × stroke), 7.6:1 c.r., 2-bbl carb, 162 bhp; 8.5:1 c.r., 4-bbl carb, 182 bhp; 292 cid (3.75 × 3.30), 4-bbl carb, 205 bhp (late 1955) **1956** 272 cid, 8.0/8.4:1 c.r., 173/176 bhp; 292 cid, 8.4:1 c.r., Holley 4-bbl carb, 200/202/205 bhp; 312 cid (3.80 × 3.44), 8.4:1 c.r., Holley 4-bbl carb, 215/225 bhp
Transmission:	3-speed manual; overdrive and 3-speed Fordomatic automatic opt.
Suspension, front:	upper and lower A-arms, coil springs,
Suspension, rear:	live axle, semi-elliptic leaf springs,
Brakes:	front/rear drums
Wheelbase (in.):	115.5
Weight (lbs):	3,081-3,566
Top speed (mph):	95-110
0-60 mph (sec):	9.5-14.0
Base price (V-8):	$1,706-$2,533
Production (Six & V-8):	**1955** Mainline 2d sdn 76,698 bus cpe 8,809 4d sdn 41,794 Customline 2d sdn 236,575 4d sdn 235,417 Fairlane Victoria htp cpe 113,372 Crown Victoria htp cpe 33,165 Crown Victoria glass-top htp cpe 1,999 2d sdn 173,311 4d sdn 254,437 Sunliner cvt 49,966 2d Ranch Wagon 40,493 2d Custom Ranch Wagon 43,671 4d 8P Country Sedan wgn 53,209 4d 6P Country Sedan wgn 53,075 4d 8P Country Squire wgn 19,011 **1956** Mainline 2d sdn 106,794 bus cpe 8,020 4d sdn 49,448 Customline 2d sdn 164,828 4d sdn 170,695 Victoria htp cpe 33,130 Fairlane Victoria htp sdn 32,111 Crown Victoria htp cpe 9,209 Crown Victoria glass-top htp cpe 603 Victoria htp cpe 177,735 2d sdn 142,629 4d sdn 224,872 Sunliner cvt 58,147 2d Ranch Wagon 48,348 2d Custom Ranch wgn 42,317 2d Parklane wgn 15,186 4d 8P Country Sedan wgn 85,374 4d 8P Country Squire wgn 23,221

Fords apparently got it, too.

As might be expected, the '56 Ford was faster than the '55: 0-60 acceleration was down to about 11.5 seconds with the 292 and Fordomatic—*Motor Trend* and *Motor Life* both did it in 11.6, *Motorsport* in 11.3—and *Speed Age* magazine managed 0-60 in 10.21 seconds with the 200-bhp 292 and overdrive. The 312 with a stick shift could do it in under 10 seconds, but then so could the 205-bhp Chevy (with just 265 cubic inches). Ford nonetheless fought it out in February at the Daytona Speed Weeks, where a strong showing in the NASCAR races gave Ford 584 points to Chevy's 566, enough to capture the Pure Oil Manufacturer's Trophy. Still, Chevy took the standing-start one-mile run at 81.39 mph to Ford's 80.84, and the flying mile at 121.33 mph versus 118.13.

Ford had become heavily involved in NASCAR in 1955, running with 205-bhp Interceptor V-8s. While they ran, they stole the show. But the cars needed more development, especially the suspensions, which gave way and handed the Southern 500 to Chevrolet. Though it couldn't match the mighty Chrysler 300s in NASCAR during 1956, Ford did manage 14 wins, including the Southern 500. But even though Chevy and Chrysler stole the spotlight in 1955-56, the top V-8 options made Fords muscle cars of their time.

1957 Ford Thunderbird

First displayed as a wood mock-up at the Detroit Auto Show in early 1954, the Thunderbird debuted as a "personal" car, *not* a sports car. It rode the same 102-inch wheelbase as the first-generation Corvette, to be sure, but put the emphasis on luxury and practicality. In place of creaking fiberglass and clumsy side curtains stood a sturdy all-steel body with convenient roll-up windows. Instead of an ill-fitting soft top came a snug power top, lift-off hard top, or both. And in place of a plodding six, the T-Bird packed a burley 292-cid Mercury V-8 good for 193/198 horsepower (stick/automatic).

Boasting European style and American comfort, convenience, and go, the Thunderbird proved well-nigh irresistible. With 16,155 built, it whipped the rival Chevy in 1955 model-year production by nearly 24 to one! You don't mess with success in Detroit, and Ford didn't with the '56 'Bird. The few changes included an exterior-mounted spare (for more trunk space), softer suspension (for a smoother ride), and optional portholes for the hardtop (for better over-the-shoulder visibility). And, of course, there was more power from a 202-bhp 292 V-8 and 215/225 horses (overdrive/Fordomatic) from a 312 V-8. If that wasn't enough, later in the model year a dual four-barrel carb option rated at 260 horsepower became available, but only for those willing to shift gears. Production eased slightly to 15,631 units, but still beat arch-rival Corvette by five to one. Trouble was, Ford wanted higher volume, and had already settled on a four-seater T-Bird for 1958 and beyond.

The '57 thus ended up being the last two-seater 'Bird—and arguably the best. A handsome facelift brought a prominent bumper/grille and a longer rear deck (again enclosing the spare) wearing modest canted tailfins.

Power soared upward, too, starting with the 292 V-8 rated at 212 bhp at 4500 rpm on 9.1:1 compression, but only with a stick shift. Of far more interest to enthusiasts was the 312 in its various "Thunderbird Special" guises: 9.7:1 compression, Holley four-barrel carb, 245 horsepower at 4500 rpm; twin Holley four-barrels, 270 bhp at 4800 rpm; and the Racing Kit with 10.0:1 compression and 285 bhp at 5000 rpm. And that wasn't all—Ford also trotted out a "Thunderbird Special Supercharged" 312 with compression lowered to 8.5:1 to accommodate the

The '57 model was destined to be the last of the two-seater T-Birds (*bottom row*). Prices started at $3408, but options added up quickly. One of the rarest was the $500 McCulloch supercharged 312 V-8 (*right*), which boasted a soul-stirring 300 horsepower at 4800 rpm. The blower delivered up to six psi of compressed air to a sealed four-throat carb, and with it 0-60 came up in less than seven seconds.

Paxton-McCulloch supercharger. Output was a towering 300 horses at 4800 rpm. And there was yet another 312, a NASCAR screamer pumping out 340 horsepower at 5300 rpm.

The blower was supplied at the behest of driver Pete DePaolo, who'd learned that Chevy might have a blower on its '57 Corvette. A $500 option, this centrifugal unit delivered up to six psi of compressed air to a sealed four-throat carb, and it did wonders for performance. While the 245-bhp setup would see 115 mph and turn 0-60 in about 9 seconds, the blown 'Bird was

good for at least 125 mph and could hit 60 mph in well under seven seconds—closer to six by some accounts. Reportedly, just 208 blower 'Birds were built, plus another 1500 units with the twin-four-barrel 270- and 285-bhp engines.

Though not considered a true sports car, T-Birds did go racing, albeit with limited success. A '55 sponsored by *Mechanix Illustrated*'s Tom McCahill, who owned the first production 'Bird, swept the production sports car class at that year's Daytona Speed Weeks, with Joe Ferguson's two-way average of 124.633 mph besting every Austin-Healey, Porsche, and all but one Jaguar

The handsome facelift accorded the '57 Thunderbird (*below*) has made it the favored "little" 'Bird among collectors. A very few '57 Fords also ended up with a supercharger under the hood, here in a lightweight Custom Tudor (*bottom*).

XK-120. Chuck Daigh did even better in 1956 with a Pete DePaolo-prepped car, running 88.779 mph in the standing mile, though Zora Arkus-Duntov's modified 'Vette prove a bit faster at 89.735 mph. In 1957, Daigh set an acceleration mark at 93.312 mph, and a privately entered T-Bird ran the flying mile at 146.282 mph one way, and averaged 138.775 mph both ways. Danny Eames, meanwhile, took his modified '57 to an acceleration mark of 97.933 mph, and made the flying-run mile at 160.356 mph. Then the Automobile Manufacturers Association issued its infamous racing "ban"—and T-Bird development stopped.

But the two-seater Thunderbird had proved its point. If not a true sports car, it could certainly be a high-performance car. That it also exuded style and luxury made it all the more remarkable—and memorable.

1957 Ford Thunderbird Major Specifications	
Engine:	ohv V-8: 292 cid (3.75 × 3.30-in. bore × stroke), 9.1:1 c.r., Holley 4-bbl carb, 212 bhp; 312 cid (3.80 × 3.44), 9.7:1 c.r., 4-bbl carb, 245 bhp; 2 Holley 4-bbl carbs, 270 bhp; Racing Kit, 10.0:1 c.r., 285 bhp; Supercharged, 8.5:1 c.r., 300 bhp; NASCAR version, 340 bhp
Transmission:	3-speed manual w/overdrive; 3-speed Fordomatic automatic
Suspension, front:	upper and lower A-arms, coil springs
Suspension, rear:	live axle, semi-elliptic leaf springs
Brakes:	front/rear drums
Wheelbase (in.):	102.0
Weight (lbs):	3,145
Top speed (mph):	120+
0-60 mph (sec):	6.5-9.0
Base price:	$3,408
Production:	21,380 (all models); 208 Supercharged (incl. 15 Daytona specials and 340-bhp models)

58

1951-54 Hudson Hornet

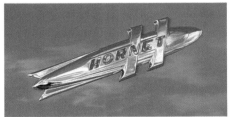

Before World War II, Hudson-powered cars had seen many competition successes at Indianapolis, at hill climbs, in record runs, and in stock-car events. In fact, Hudson owned 149 AAA (American Automobile Association) prewar records.

Hudson's new postwar models were destined to become the basis for the make's greatest racing triumphs. The rakish '48s rode a 124-inch-wheelbase "Step-down" design that was much wider than high—77 versus 60 inches. Construction was unitized, with the main structural members located below door level so the floor was lower than the door sills. The suspension system featured front and rear stabilizer bars and splayed rear leaf springs. All this made for the lowest center of gravity in the industry and outstanding handling compared to narrower, higher rivals.

Oldsmobile raised the performance standard in the medium-price field with its 1949 overhead-valve V-8. With 135 bhp from 303.7 cubes in the light 88, Olds fielded the fastest car in its class. Hudson, meanwhile, had put its bucks into the new-for-'48 262-cid "Super Six." In 1951, it was enlarged to 308 cid, making it the biggest production six around—and exclusive to the Hornet. Dubbed H-145, it had a two-barrel carb and 145 horsepower. Buyers could choose from a 6.7:1 or 7.2:1 compression head, though no extra power was claimed for the latter. Chrysler's FirePower V-8 and the new Studebaker V-8 also bowed for '51, so the Hornet's old fashioned L-head six

Even the most powerful early Fifties V-8s felt the sting of the Hornet (*left*). A rare body style of Hudson's new NASCAR champ was the '51 Hollywood hardtop, of which an estimated 2100 were built. Riding a 124-inch wheelbase, it weighed 3630 pounds and sold for $2869, just $182 less than a Buick Roadmaster Riviera hardtop.

wasn't exactly the center of attention.

However, it *did* attract the attention of Daytona Beach garage operator Marshall Teague. A master at tuning and driving race cars, he felt the Hornet could be competitive in the 160-mile stock-car race to be held in his hometown in February. So he bought one, set it up, painted "Fabulous Hudson Hornet" on its sides—and won.

Encouraged, Teague traveled to Detroit searching for heavy-duty parts to make the Hornet go faster and last longer. Both the engineering and advertising departments were receptive; Hudson needed something to drum up interest in its rapidly aging cars. A deal was struck: Teague would get help on the parts he needed; in return, he would do PR work for Hudson.

"Severe usage" items soon began showing up on Hudson parts lists, the most visible being Twin-H Power. Using two equally spaced carburetors for better air/fuel distribution, an old hot-rodding trick, Teague knew it would increase power. Hudson even had the hardware lying around, so Twin-H became a Hornet option in late 1951. As the racing season progressed, many drivers switched to Hudson feeling it had the hot setup for big and small tracks alike. Because of an earlier start, however, Olds held sway in total wins: 20 NASCAR Grand National victories to Hudson's 12. On another front, Teague finished sixth overall in November 1951 in the car-killing, 2000-mile *Carrera Panamericana* (Mexican Road Race), run mostly on dirt roads. The Hornet actually held the Ferraris on the fast bends, to the "Carambas!" of spectators.

Hudson was ready for 1952. Twin-H became a full production option (but had no horsepower rating), and with more drivers in Hudsons the year turned out to be the Hornet's best. Tim Flock won the NASCAR Grand National crown, and 27 of the 34 scheduled events fell to Hudson. Oldsmobile? A mere three. Teague raced the AAA circuit, taking half of the 14 AAA stock wins; other Hudson drivers took five more, giving the Hornet a total of 39 wins in 48 major races.

Winning didn't mean Hudson could slack off, so a hotter engine—the 7-X—joined the parts list for dealer installation. It had an overbored block capped by a high-compression head, plus split exhaust manifolding. Horsepower wasn't divulged, but it was believed to be around 210. Competition was tougher in 1953, leaving Hudson with 22 wins in 37 NASCAR starts, with Thomas regaining the championship. Olds took nine, Dodge six. At AAA, Hornets nabbed 13 of 16 races.

NASCAR banned all factory-authorized parts for 1954, but this actually helped Hudson. True, the competition had some powerful engines, like Chrysler's 235-bhp FirePower V-8, but without the "authorized" handling parts they were no match for the agile Hornets, which were now up to 160 bhp (170 with Twin-H) in stock form. But

though other makes were catching up, Hudson still won 17 of 36 NASCAR Grand Nationals—more than any other make for the third straight year. Olds settled for 11 wins, Chrysler seven.

Though Hudson was king of the racing world, sales were plummeting. The old Step-down body was seven years old in 1954, and there was no money to replace it or to develop a V-8, increasingly demanded by a power-hungry public. On May 1, 1954, Hudson and Nash-Kelvinator merged to form American Motors. As a result, Hudson's Detroit factory was closed, ending the saga of one of the greatest stock-car racers of all time.

NEW LOW PRICE
FOR THE NATIONAL CHAMPION

Winner of more stock-car events than all other makes combined!

New HUDSON HORNET SPECIAL

HUDSON DIVISION OF AMERICAN MOTORS

60

The most popular '51 Hornet was the $2568 four-door sedan (*opposite, top*). It ran with Hudson's Super Six engine enlarged to 308 cubic inches (*opposite, center*) and kicked out 145 horsepower, 10 more than Oldsmobile's ohv V-8. The '53 Hornet showed only trim differences; the four-door (*left*) listed at $2769, the club coupe (*center*) at $2742. For '54, the Hornet received its most extensive facelift. Seen here is the $3288 Brougham convertible (*bottom*), along with its "Twin H-Power" badge. A cheaper Hornet Special was advertised in 1954 (*opposite, bottom*), but it didn't help plummeting sales, nor in the long run did the Hornet's impressive racing successes.

1951-54 Hudson Hornet Major Specifications

Engines:	L-head I-6, 308 cid (3.81 × 4.50-in. bore × stroke), chrome alloy block, 7.2:1 c.r., Carter 2-bbl carb
	1951-53 6.7:1 c.r. (7.2:1 opt.), 145/160 bhp (standard/Twin-H)
	1954 7.5:1 c.r., 160/170 bhp (standard/Twin-H)
	7-X racing engine 341.0 cid (4.01 × 4.50), approx. 210 bhp
Transmission:	3-speed manual; overdrive and 4-speed GM Hydra-Matic opt.
Suspension, front:	upper transverse beam, lower A-arms, coil springs, anti-roll bar
Suspension, rear:	live axle, splayed semi-elliptic leaf springs, anti-roll bar
Brakes:	front/rear drums
Wheelbase (in.):	124.0
Weight (lbs):	3,505-3,800
Top speed (mph):	98-110
0-60 mph (sec):	12.0-14.5
Base price:	$2,543-$3,342
Production:	**1951** 43,656 **1952** 35,921
	1953 27,208 **1954** 24,833

1952-55 Lincoln

In 1950, a reporter asked Ford Motor Company chief engineer Harold Youngren when he thought there'd be a new Lincoln. "Soon, please God," he replied. The answer to Youngren's prayer arrived for 1952, and it was remarkable: smooth, curvy in the right places, and clean. The hood sat a bit below front-fender level for excellent forward vision, and rear fenders with a forward-raked dummy scoop and large taillights provided visual interest.

All '52 Lincolns rode a 123-inch wheelbase, a compromise between the previous 121/125-inch spans. Cosmopolitan now denoted the standard line, Capri the upper-class cars—and both series listed Lincoln's first pillarless hardtop.

Engineering changes were dramatic. They started with engineer Earle S. MacPherson's new ball-joint front suspension, with rotating sockets instead of conventional kingpins and bushings

that eliminated lots of unsprung weight and 12 of 16 grease fittings. The result was a Lincoln with a fine ride and surprisingly good handling. Said *Motor Trend:* "It doesn't heel excessively on sharp, high-speed turns, and it doesn't feel like you're guiding a couple of sponges around a turn." Also new were recirculating-ball power steering, oversize drum brakes, more and better body mounts, and improved insulation for quietness and solidity.

But the capper was a brand-new V-8, Lincoln's first valve-in-head powerplant, and superior to its rivals in many ways. Its crankshaft, for example, had eight counterweights instead of the usual six, plus oversize intake valves for better breathing and more output per cubic inch. Also featured was a deep-skirted crankcase extending below the crank centerline for an extremely stiff shaft support. Unlike the old flathead, the new V-8 was a short-stroke, oversquare design displacing 317.5 cubic inches. Horsepower was 160 with standard two-barrel carb and 7.5:1 compression. GM's dual-range four-speed Hydra-Matic was the only transmission offered.

This fast, roadable package seemed tailor-made for competition; tuning whiz Clay Smith, helped by a bin full of heavy-duty "export" parts, made it an outstanding performer in the 1952 *Carrera Panamericana* (Mexican Road Race). Running the length of Mexico, the event was as much a test of stamina as speed. Seeking the best results, the Lincoln team drove 1953 models, shown well ahead of public introduction. Bill Stroppe and ace mechanic Clay Smith prepared three cars, with Indy veterans Chuck Stevenson, Johnny Mantz, and Walt Faulkner doing the driving. Not only did the well-prepped Lincolns finish 1-2-3 in the new "American Stock" class, stock-car driver Bob Korf, piloting an independent Lincoln entered by outboard motor industrialist Carl Kiekhaefer, capped the triumph by finishing fourth. Overall, the Lincolns placed right behind six high-priced European sports cars.

Styling and chassis adjustments were minor for '53, but a host of engine tweaks—higher 8.0:1 compression, four-barrel Holley carb, bigger intake valves, better manifolding, higher-lift cam—boosted horsepower to 205. Tom McCahill of *Mechanix Illustrated* had panned the '52 Lincoln for

The '52 Lincoln was one of the few truly "all-new" cars the public ever gets to see. The 123-inch chassis was new, the body above it was new, the ball-joint suspension beneath it was new, and the 317.5-cubic-inch overhead-valve V-8 that powered it was new. The result was one of the most roadable big cars ever placed on the market. Styling was fresh and crisp, as seen on the $3665 Capri convertible (*opposite page*), of which only 1191 were built. *This page:* Its 160-bhp V-8 (*left*) boasted many new features. The $3549 '53 Capri hardtop (*above*) attracted 12,916 buyers, while the '54 Capri ragtop, which cost $4031, found 1951 takers.

lack of power, but glowed after testing the '53: "The Lincoln is far ahead of any immediate American competitor in roadability and cornering....I can honestly state the 1953 Lincoln is America's finest automobile." He backed it up by buying one. And despite having to run "more stock," Lincoln had another fine year in Mexico as Stevenson, Walt Faulkner, Jack McGrath, and Johnny Mantz finished 1-4 in class and 6-9 overall against everything from race-bred sports cars to Hemi Chryslers to Henry Js.

The '54s changed little mechanically, but a heavier grille and more bright-work made them look richer. With 212, 230, and 235 horsepower, Packard, Ca-

For '55, Lincoln's major facelift gave it longer rear fenders, plus new taillights and reworked grille. But most cars wore all-new styling—and Lincoln didn't even have a wraparound windshield! Still, the restyle was a handsome one, hinting at the looks of the '56 Lincoln. Whether Lincoln's racing success in the *Carrera Panamericana* actually helped sales became a moot point, because 1955 was a transition year as Lincoln began to move to larger, more luxurious cars. They would still perform well, but racing would no longer be part of the Lincoln mystique.

dillac, and Chrysler were more powerful, but Lincoln again had Mexico to crow about. For that year's race, new 1954 cars were prepared, all two-door hardtops as before. There were now five classes: two for sports cars and three for stocks. This fifth—and last—*Carrera* saw Lincoln's third consecutive sweep, with Faulkner trailing privateer Ray Crawford in the International Stock Class behind a pack of sports cars. However, the factory team wasn't as successful against the tougher opposition. Of 14 cars entered, half by the factory, only four finished, including two privateers. For Lincoln, it was perhaps fortunate that the fabled road race ended when it did.

Lincoln suffered in the red-hot '55 sales race, mainly because it wasn't as "new" as that year's rivals. It didn't even have a wraparound windshield! But it was still a top-quality item—and more powerful than ever thanks to a newly bored 341 V-8 with 225 bhp. An important image point was the arrival of Lincoln's own automatic, three-speed Turbo-Drive. Yet despite the changes and its road-race heritage, Lincoln was one of the few makes to see sales slip for '55. But it was only temporary: Lincoln would bounce back with a larger and trendier car for '56, leaving its racing successes a matter of history.

1952-55 Lincoln Major Specifications

Engine:	ohv V-8 **1952** 317.5 cid (3.80 × 3.50-in. bore × stroke), 7.5:1 c.r., Holley 2-bbl carb, 160 bhp **1953-54** 8.0:1 c.r., Holley 4-bbl carb, 205 bhp **1955** 341 cid (3.94 × 3.50), 8.5:1 c.r., 225 bhp
Transmission:	**1952-54** 4-speed GM Hydra-Matic **1955** 3-speed Turbo-Drive automatic
Suspension, front:	upper and lower A-arms, coil springs
Suspension, rear:	live axle, semi-elliptic leaf springs
Brakes:	front/rear drums
Wheelbase (in.):	123.0
Weight (lbs):	4,125-4,415
Top speed (mph):	105-115
0-60 mph (sec):	11.0-13.0
Base price:	$3,198-$4,072
Production:	**1952 Cosmopolitan** Sport Coupe 2d htp 4,545 4d sdn 15,854 (incl. Capri) **Capri** Sport Coupe 2d htp 5,681 4d sdn (incl. with Cosmo sedan) cvt 1,191 **1953 Cosmopolitan** Sport Coupe 2d htp 6,562 4d sdn 7,560 **Capri** Sport Coupe 2d htp 12,916 4d sdn 11,352 cvt 2,372 **1954 Cosmopolitan** Sport Coupe 2d htp 2,994 4d sdn 4,447 **Capri** Sport Coupe 2d htp 14,003 4d sdn 13,598 cvt 1,951 **1955 Custom** Sport Coupe 2d htp 1,362 4d sdn 2,187 **Capri** Sport Coupe 2d htp 11,462 4d sdn 10,724 cvt 1,487

1956 Mercury

Mercury was a car bred for performance. Bowing for 1939, its mission was to get a slice of the lower-medium-price market that Ford Motor Company had been missing. Slightly bigger and heavier than the Ford V-8, it also got a larger 239-cid flathead rated at 95 bhp, so it developed a reputation as a hot car.

Postwar saw new styling for 1949, a more modern chassis, and a 255.4-cid V-8 good for 110 horses. Mercury won two NASCAR races in both 1950 and '51 with this engine, but it was really no match for the Olds 88 or Hudson Hornet on the track. Meanwhile, a compression boost from 6.8:1 to 7.2:1 brought 125 horses for 1952-53. When Mercury's new overhead-valve V-8 finally arrived for 1954, it proved nothing to get excited about. Displacement stayed about the same, a modest 256 cubic inches, though horsepower did increase to 161. Also new for '54 was

ball-joint front suspension, a boon to handling.

The '55 models signaled that Mercury wanted to recapture its early performance image. Engine displacement now stood at 292 cubes with 188 bhp from 7.6:1 compression, plus an extra 10 horses with an 8.5:1 squeeze. Bodies wore a combination of old and new styling: The grille carried on the 1954 theme, but rooflines were different, as was the wraparound windshield. Lincoln-Mercury Division had been a winner in the heavy-stock class in the *Carrera Panamericana*, while Dodge Hemi V-8s were cleaning up in the light-stock class. With a decent suspension and adequate power, Mercury wanted to do something about that, so builder Bill Stroppe was recruited to prepare a few '55 cars for the event which he did by beefing up the suspension and tweeking the engines. When the Mexican government cancelled the *Carrera*,

At Mercury, 1956 was the year of "THE BIG M." This was announced boldly on the hood, and there were changes underneath it to back up the advertising hype. The Custom ragtop cost $2712.

division boss Benson Ford said to race the things somewhere, so Stroppe put together a team for AAA (American Automobile Association) stock-car events. Though Mercury managed one win in a 250-miler at Milwaukee, Chrysler took 10 out of the 13 races.

Displacement rose to 312 cubes for the facelifted '56s. Initially, 225 bhp was to be tops, but as you could get that in a Ford, the "Big M" needed more. This turned up as a mid-year option with a pair of four-barrel carbs and a kick in compression to 9.75:1, which rendered 260 horsepower. Appropriately named M-260, the setup was heralded by small

1956 Mercury Major Specifications	
Engine:	ohv V-8, 312 cid (3.80 × 3.44-in. bore × stroke), 4-bbl carb: 8.0:1 c.r., 210 bhp; 8.4:1 c.r., 215 bhp; 9.0:1 c.r., 225/235 bhp **M-260 V-8** 9.75:1 c.r., 2 4-bbl carbs, 260 bhp
Transmission:	3-speed manual; overdrive and 3-speed Merc-O-Matic automatic opt.
Suspension, front:	upper and lower A-arms, coil springs
Suspension, rear:	live axle, semi-elliptic leaf springs
Brakes:	front/rear drums
Wheelbase (in.):	119.0
Weight (lbs):	3,430-3,885
Top speed (mph):	105-115
0-60 mph (sec):	9.0-11.0
Base price:	$2,254-$2,977
Production: Medalist Phaeton htp sdn 6,685 Sport htp cpe 11,892 **2d sdn** 20,582 **4d sdn** 6,653 **Custom Phaeton htp sdn** 12,187 **Sport htp cpe** 20,857 **2d sdn** 16,343 **4d sdn** 15,860 **cvt** 2,311 **4d wgn 8P** 9,292 **4d wgn 6P** 8,478 **Monterey Phaeton htp sdn** 10,726 **4d Sport Sedan** 11,765 **Sport htp cpe** 42,863 **4d sdn** 26,735 **4d wgn 8P** 13,280 **Montclair Phaeton htp sdn** 23,493 **4d Sport Sedan** 9,617 **Sport htp cpe** 50,562 **cvt** 7,762	

Big difference in THE BIG M
more **usable** horsepower!

For 1956_the big move is to THE BIG **MERCURY**

All '56 Mercurys were energized by a 312 V-8, which in the Custom shown here cranked out 210 or 225 horsepower, the first with the rarely chosen stick shift, the second with the much more popular Merc-O-Matic. In mid-year, the M-260, a 260-horse 312 with a 9.75:1 squeeze and twin four-barrel carbs became an option for all models. The '56 brochure hyped "THE BIG M"—in bold capital letters—while ads talked about the "usable" power from its "SAFETY-SURGE V-8."

chrome plates on the front fenders. Further, it was available for all models, as was Dodge's D-500 setup, also advertised at 260 bhp.

Bill Stroppe was retained to prep '56 Merc stockers for both NASCAR and USAC (United States Auto Club) circuits. (USAC replaced AAA in 1956.) The fireworks started at the Daytona Beach Speed Weeks. With three Monterey two-door hardtops to do battle in the flying-mile and oval-track race, Stroppe arrived amidst the publicity surrounding DeSoto's 138-mph flying-mile run in the factory-experimental class. Determined to beat it, he bought a new Custom two-door hardtop from a local dealer and outfitted it with a roll bar, Indy-type magnesium wheels, special Firestone tires, and a Lincoln V-8 bored out to 391 cubes and fitted with fuel injection. With a couple of internal tricks, he had his own factory experimental, the JT-450X. He even gave it large lettering to be sure it attracted attention. Despite troubles on the second run, Stroppe's car averaged 147.26 mph, topping its class. The JT-450X then toured the show circuit, making demonstration runs at tracks where the factory Mercurys raced.

In the '56 Daytona 160-miler, Billy Myers finished first in class, but second to winner Tim Flock in a Chrysler 300-B. Though Mercury copped only five NASCAR wins that season, it came to the fore by setting 20 new world records in NASCAR-sponsored Speed Trials at Kingman, Arizona.

Out in the real world, *Motor Trend* found that a 225-bhp '56 Montclair with Merc-O-Matic would tackle the 0-60 sprint in 11 seconds, 30-50 in 4.5, and 50-80 in about 12. *MT* also said that "we haven't found a better road car in '56." Tom McCahill of *Mechanix Illustrated* obtained similar results, noting a top speed of 108-111 mph. The 260-bhp 312 easily pushed the benchmark 0-60 time to well under 10 seconds.

When all was said and done, the '56 Merc held its ground as one of Detroit's hottest cars. "As reliable as Judgement Day and as chic as a Paris original," said McCahill. "Here is a car loaded with looks, stamina and performance...a mink coat at a muskrat price."

1950 Oldsmobile Futuramic 88

The original Oldsmobile 88 can lay fair claim as America's first post-war "muscle car," sounding the gun for the "horsepower race" of the Fifties. It was definitely a hit. Despite being a last-minute addition, the debut 1949 models sold more than 99,000 copies. The evolutionary '50s racked up over a quarter-million orders. Just as quickly, the 88 began compiling an enviable competition record that firmly endowed Olds with a high-performance image that would prove a key factor in that make's consistently high sales for most of the decade. With all this, the 88 deserves its longstanding place in the automotive hall of fame.

Like many good ideas, the 88 concept was disarmingly simple. Olds shared 1949 honors with sister division Cadillac for the industry's first high-compression overhead-valve V-8. At first, Oldsmobile's new 303.7-cubic-inch "Rocket" engine was to be

limited to the senior C-body 98 series that, again with Cadillac, had ushered in General Motors' first new postwar styling the previous year. With the new look being extended to the company's junior A- and B-body models for 1949, Olds general manager Sherrod Skinner conceived the brilliant notion of slotting the compact, 135-horsepower V-8 into his lighter, Chevy-size Series 76 that still trundled around with a 105-bhp six. Voilà! Instant excitement.

The result came as a revelation to buyers accustomed to plodding L-head sixes and slow-revving straight eights. Weighing 300-500 pounds less than a 98, the typical 88 had a power-to-weight ratio of about 22.5:1, not so hot by late-Fifties standards perhaps, but sufficient to make this one of the quickest cars you could find on any showroom floor. And with prices as low as $2143 for the standard-trim fastback

The '50 Oldsmobile "ROCKET" V-8 (*above*) was promoted as "THE POWER SENSATION OF THE NATION." "This is truly the engine of the future," Olds proclaimed, "and it's here today—more brilliant than ever!" Also brilliant was the new Deluxe 88 Holiday hardtop (*top*), a $2267 offering. The sparser base Holiday listed at $2162.

club coupe, the 88 offered more go for the dough than anything else on the road.

And the new Rocket V-8 was a gem, with an impressive 263 pounds/feet torque at a low 1800 rpm, sturdy five-main-bearing crankshaft, modern oversquare bore/stroke dimensions, and tremendous internal strength. Though initially running on a mild 7.25:1 compression ratio, it could go as high as 12.0:1. Mated to the 88's V-8 was GM's four-speed "Whirlaway" Hydra-Matic, though a three-speed stick would be available on the 1950 88.

There weren't many auto enthusiast publications in 1949, but there *was* a new stock-car sanctioning body in Daytona Beach, Florida, the National Association for Stock Car Auto Racing (NASCAR). Operated by former race driver Bill France, it sought to bring organization to the sport, and promote competition among new production cars. Accordingly, a race for the late-models was held on the oval track at Daytona, consisting of part paved road and part beach. Red Byron won the event in a '49 88. Of the nine races held that year, all called Grand Nationals, Oldsmobile took five (two by Byron), leaving two to Lincoln and one to Plymouth. Byron scored the most points, thus becoming the first Grand National champion; runner-up Bob Flock also drove an 88. In addition, a 1949 Oldsmobile convertible, with Wilbur Shaw at the wheel, paced the Indianapolis 500, giving further exposure to the new star of the performance world.

The following year, an 88 broke the class record at Daytona with a two-way average of 100.28 mph. Also in 1950, an 88 won its class in the first *Carrera Panamericana* Mexican Road Race, besting rivals such as Alfa Romeo, Cadillac, and Lincoln. On the ovals, 88s took 10 of 19 contests in 1950 and 20 of 41 in 1951. Though displaced by the amazing six-cylinder Hudson Hornet in 1952-54, the 88 continued to show its ability—and stamina. A 1950 model nicknamed "Roarin' Relic" was still winning the occasional modified-class stock-car race as late as 1959.

Such goings-on naturally helped Olds' sales after the postwar seller's market peaked in 1950, when the division built nearly 408,000 cars for the model year—its second consecutive record, and one that wouldn't be exceeded until 1955.

Model year 1950 brought minor styl-

Among the range of body styles Olds listed for the Futuramic 88 in 1950 (*opposite, bottom left*) was the fastback Club Sedan, here the $2301 Deluxe (*opposite, top*). The convertible (*above*) listed at $2559, while the notchback club coupe (*right*) started at $2143. Some Olds dealers even used factory-approved see-through hoods to highlight the new V-8 (*above right*). The '88's "road-hugging chassis" provided an "Air-Borne Ride" (*opposite, bottom right*), emphasized by a jet plane flying in the background. Other ads (*bottom right*) implored prospects to "Make a Date with a 'Rocket 8'!"

ing changes to a "Futuramic 88" line that expanded via Harley Earl's pillarless hardtop coupe body style, which Olds called Holiday. Standard and Deluxe versions were offered at $2162 and $2267, respectively. Olds began giving up on fastback sedans much sooner than, say, Chevy, dropping its four-door Town Sedan this year. For 1951 it would abandon the slope-roof two-door Club Sedan as well.

Otherwise, 88 offerings for 1950 repeated those of '49: convertible, club coupe, two- and four-door notchback sedans, and four-door wagon. All but the ragtop came in Standard and Deluxe form, the latter typically costing $78 more. Prices ranged from the basic $1904 Club Sedan—about $375 more than a two-door Ford V-8—to $2662 for the Deluxe wagon.

The Fifties would see a lot of fast Oldsmobiles, but the 88 was the first— and that makes it special. Today it's revered as the granddaddy of modern muscle.

1950 Oldsmobile Futuramic 88 Major Specifications

Engine:	ohv V-8, 303.7 cid (3.75 × 3.44-in. bore × stroke), 7.25:1 c.r., 2-bbl carb, 135 bhp
Transmission:	3-speed manual, 4-speed "Whirlaway" Hydra-Matic automatic opt.
Suspension, front:	upper and lower A-arms, coil springs, lever shocks
Suspension, rear:	live axle, coil springs, lever shocks
Brakes:	front/rear drums
Wheelbase (in.):	119.5
Weight (lbs):	3,435-3,780
Top speed (mph):	97
0-60 mph (sec):	12.0-13.5
Production:	**2d Club Sedan** 14,705
	Deluxe 2d Club Sedan 16,388
club cpe 10,684	**Deluxe club cpe** 10,772
cvt 9,127	**Holiday 2d htp** 1,366
	Deluxe Holiday 2d htp 11,316
4d sdn 40,301	**Deluxe 4d sdn** 100,810
2d sdn 23,889	**Deluxe 2d sdn** 26,672
4d wgn 1,830	**Deluxe 4d wgn** 552

1955 Oldsmobile Super 88

The 1954-56 Oldsmobiles were arguably Lansing's best efforts of the decade: smooth and solid per Olds tradition, flashy in the spirit of the times yet not overdone, surprisingly roadable. They certainly ranked as the most popular Oldsmobiles of the '50s. Consider that the division rose from sixth to fifth in industry sales with its '54 line, then claimed fourth on 1955 volume of 583,179 units—a record that would stand for the next decade.

As before, the senior Ninety-Eight employed the GM C-body, the midrange Super 88 and base 88 series the corporate B-body. Wheelbases went up two inches across the board—to 122 and 126 inches—with the advent of a new X-member frame that helped reduce overall height and center of gravity. New-type front coil springs and repositioned rear springs and shocks aided handling. Performance improved via a bored-out 324.3-cid Rocket V-8 with higher 8.25:1 compression, good for 170 horsepower with two-barrel

carb for the 88 and 185 bhp in four-barrel form for Super 88 and Ninety-Eight. The extra power was welcome, as curb weights rose some 80-120 pounds, though surprisingly the lightest 1954 88 was only 150 pounds heavier than the lightest 1949 88.

"Uncle" Tom McCahill of *Mechanix Illustrated* spoke of "whip-lashing dash" after testing the Super 88. "In showroom tune it will push the Buick Century right to the wire," he said. Though manual shift was standard on 88s and Super 88s, most Oldsmobiles left the factory with Hydra-Matic, which *Motor Trend* praised as "one of the smoothest-shifting ... we've ever tested."

Styling refinements and new four-door hardtop models were 1955 highlights, but the big news was still more power for the "horsepower race": 185 for the 88, 202 for the Super 88 and Ninety-Eight (optional on the 88). Olds did it via a higher-lift cam, larger and stronger exhaust valves, new-design

combustion chambers, cooler-running spark plugs, and tighter 8.5:1 compression. *Motor Trend* called the 88s "family hot rods, one of the industry's top combinations of performance, long life span, and style." Nor was roadability neglected, as the front suspension gained direct-acting shocks, a new stabilizer bar, and recalibrated coil springs.

An attractive facelift and more power marked the '56 Oldsmobiles. Another round of internal changes—revised carburetion, new intake manifold, larger exhaust valves, still-higher compression (9.25:1)—brought output to an unprecedented 230/240 bhp, and a second Hydra-Matic option, called "Jetaway," offered a second fluid coupling and smoother shifting. A "bigmouth" grille and simpler side trim provided model-year identification, but you had to look fast because a Super 88 could do 0-60 in under 11 seconds. Road tests of a '54 and '55 Super 88 four-door sedan reported 0-60 times of 12.4 and 10.6 seconds, while a heavi-

After an all-new Olds for '54, the '55 received a facelift with a smarter grille and splashier bodyside two-toning. The Super 88 lineup included a convertible (*opposite page and left*); at $2894 it was the priciest model in that series. Just as glitzy as the exterior was the interior (*center*), also with jazzy two-toning and a chrome-laden dash. Powering the Super 88 was a 324.3-cid V-8 (*bottom*), which with 8.5:1 compression and a four-barrel carb developed 202 lively horses.

er '56 Super 88 four-door hardtop needed 10.8 seconds.

NASCAR reacted to all the trick racing stuff from the factories by banning it for 1954, going back to stock (more or less) equipment. Olds drivers managed 11 wins, their best year since 1951, but Hudson was still on top with 17. By 1956, the competition had clearly caught up with the Rocket. With average weights pushing 3800 pounds and average horsepower, Oldsmobiles were more in the mainstream of medium-priced cars than in the forefront. For example, that year you could get a Dodge with 295 bhp, a DeSoto with 320, a Mercury with 260, and even a Pontiac with 285.

Only a single NASCAR Grand National win went to Olds in 1956. And in the rapidly rising sport of drag racing, only the older 88s did well in the lower stock classes. But no matter, out on the streets in everyday driving an Oldsmobile Super 88 was still considered fast, and pretty flashy, too—a winning combination in 1955.

1955 Oldsmobile Super 88 Major Specifications

Engine:	ohv V-8, 324.3 cid (3.88 × 3.44-in. bore × stroke), 8.5:1 c.r., 4-bbl carb, 202 bhp
Transmission:	3-speed manual; Hydra-Matic opt.
Suspension, front:	upper and lower A-arms, coil springs
Suspension, rear:	live axle, semi-elliptic leaf springs
Brakes:	front/rear drums
Wheelbase (in.):	122.0
Weight (lbs):	3,720-3,983
Top speed (mph):	105-110
0-60 mph (sec):	10.5-11.5
Base price:	$2,436-$2,894
Production:	Super 88 2d sdn 11,950
	4d sdn 111,316
	Deluxe Holiday htp cpe 62,534
	Deluxe Holiday htp sdn 47,385
	cvt cpe 9,007

1957 Oldsmobile J-2

Oldsmobile, like Buick, seemed to go astray in 1957-58, the result of a conservative—if not downright complacent—attitude brought on by the huge success of 1954-56.

Billed as the most completely changed Oldsmobiles in 20 years, the "Golden Rocket" '57s came in a little longer, noticeably lower, and somewhat wider than the '56s. Wheelbases went unchanged, but spanned all-new B- and C-bodies shared with Buick. The chassis was also new: a low-riding "cowbelly" design with widely spaced side rails and Oldsmobile's first ball-joint suspension. Curb weights tacked on some 220-300 pounds, but more cubic inches took care of that, and Olds had 'em in a Rocket V-8 punched out to 371.1 cubic inches, the biggest among GM passenger cars. That mill developed 277 horsepower for all models—the first time since 1951 that the same engine had been standard across the Olds line.

Styling was relatively clean for a '57 GM car, and still unmistakably Olds. The "big-mouth" grille of 1956, flat-

tened now to full width, was shorn of its vertical divider and filled with a fine mesh instead of deeply inset horizontal bars. Bright sweepspears still dropped from the notch in the beltline to just below mid-body, but now shot straight back as in 1954. High-set "rocket" taillamps, an Olds trademark since 1950, gave way to semi-oval units with hooded tops that hinted at fins. As at Buick, sedans and hardtops sported three-piece rear windows, with curved triangular sections outboard of a wide center pane. Curious stamped ridges ran the length of the roof and down through the rear window divider pillars in some models.

Not everyone approved, but at least it looked different.

Lansing's big '57 performance news was coded J-2, a triple-carburetor package with special intake manifold, 10.0:1 compression (versus the standard 9.5:1), and new air cleaner, throttle linkage, and head gaskets. Like Dodge's D-500 option, this 300-horsepower extra could be had on any model, either factory- or dealer-installed, right down to the cheapest and lightest two-door 88—which is where the speed demons wanted it anyway. Cost? Just $83, a fraction of what rivals charged for fuel injection or supercharging. The J-2 was a genuine performance bargain, reducing the typical 0-60-mph time to a shade over nine seconds. A second J-2 kit intended for drag and stock-car racers pumped out 312 horses, but it wasn't recommended for street use, and its $395 price kept it rare.

To showcase its new-found muscle, Olds signed veteran stock-car ace Lee Petty to race 88s in NASCAR. He obliged by blasting one to nearly 145

The "Most exciting engine development since the first Rocket was launched," boasted Olds (*opposite, bottom*). And indeed, the 300-horse J-2 option made the '57 88 Holiday (*opposite, top and this page, top*) feel like it was rocket propelled. Benefiting from the J-2's extra 23 bhp was the 4364-pound Super 88 Fiesta wagon (*left*), a four-door hardtop. As Olds implored (*above*), "Join the Fun!"

Oldsmobile called the 1957 88s and Super 88s Golden Rockets, and one look at the block of the triple two-barrel carb engine (*left*) suggests why. Also featured was a 10.0:1 compression ratio, which helped pump the horsepower to 300—every one of which demanded high-octane fuel to keep them happy. The Golden Rocket 88 Holiday (*above*) came in at $2854 base, but the fender skirts cost extra.

mph on the sands at Daytona. But before the car could really prove itself, NASCAR banned multi-carb setups, fuel injection, and superchargers, forcing all stockers to run with four-barrel carbs. Then the manufacturers pulled out of racing. Petty bought leftover racing parts for a song, having decided to race the cars on his own. Five events went to Oldsmobiles in 1957 Grand National competition.

But such exploits did little for sales, and Olds lost ground for '57, retaining fifth place but on 25 percent lower volume—384,390 units. In a reflection of the start of a sharp national recession that year, the standard 88 outsold the Super 88 for the first time, and by a hefty margin: better than 40,000 units.

Things went from bad to worse as the recession deepened, and the overchromed '58 Oldsmobiles—now Dynamic 88, Super 88, and Ninety-Eight—did nothing to help. On the other hand, all Olds engines had 10.0:1 compression and the J-2 package was still nominally available, rated at 312 bhp, but the glow was off the performance market.

Strangely, one of the biggest Oldsmobile wins of all time came nearly two years after the make left racing. Lee Petty had pooled his remaining racing parts to concoct a 1959 Olds two-door hardtop. He entered it in the first Daytona 500 in 1959 on the new 2½-mile speedway and, in a literal photo finish, won. Olds earned four NASCAR wins that year, but during the season Petty switched to Plymouth. Lee won the driving crown again, but Olds could only take part of the credit.

Olds would continue to build powerful, fast cars, but any real concentration on performance or racing would have to await the arrival of the mid-size 1964 4-4-2.

1957 Oldsmobile J-2 Major Specifications

Engine:	ohv V-8, 371.1 cid (4.00 × 3.69-in. bore × stroke), 10.0:1 c.r., 3 2-bbl carbs, 300 bhp; Racing J-2 V-8, 312 bhp
Transmission:	3-speed manual; Jetaway Hydra-Matic opt.
Suspension, front:	upper and lower A-arms, coil springs
Suspension, rear:	live axle, semi-elliptic leaf springs
Brakes:	front/rear drums
Wheelbase (in.):	**88 and Super 88** 122.0 **98** 126.0
Weight (lbs):	3,942-4,572
Top speed:	110-125
0-60 mph (sec):	9.0-10.0
Base price:	$2,733-$4,217
Production:	**Golden Rocket 88 2d sdn** 18,477 **Holiday htp cpe** 49,187 **Holiday htp sdn** 33,830 **cvt cpe** 6,423 **4d sdn** 53,923 **Fiesta wgn 4d** 5,052 **Fiesta htp wgn 4d** 5,767 **Golden Rocket Super 88 Holiday htp cpe** 31,155 **Holiday htp sdn** 39,162 **cvt cpe** 7,128 **4d sdn** 42,629 **Fiesta htp wgn 4d** 8,981 **2d sdn** 2,983 **Starfire 98 Holiday htp cpe** 17,791 **Holiday htp sdn** 32,099 **cvt cpe** 8,278 **4d sdn** 21,525

1955-56 Packard Caribbean

Before World War II, there was a direct correlation between a car's horsepower and its price. This tradition continued in the immediate postwar years. Accordingly, the prestigious Packard led the horsepower list for 1946-48 with its big straight eight, and tied for the lead in 1949-50.

Packard's first V-8 didn't arrive until the 1955 model year. It came in two sizes: 320 cubic inches and a bored-out 352-cid version, the latter with the largest displacement in the industry. The overhead-valve engine was of modern design, but like the old straight eight was quite heavy—and durable—like the cars it powered. The lower-priced Clipper models came with the 320-cid unit, rated at 225 bhp with four-barrel carb. Clipper Customs used the 352 in 245-bhp form. In the senior Packards it was rated at a healthy 260 bhp, enough according to *Motor Trend* to propel a 4250-pound Four Hundred hardtop from 0-60 mph in 11.4 seconds and through the quarter-mile in 18.6 seconds at 76.3 mph.

As with the limited-production Eldorado convertible at Cadillac, the 1953-54 Caribbean ragtop had served as Packard's flagship. In 1953 it had been powered by a 327-cid straight-eight boasting 180 horsepower and nine main bearings, but this was up to 359 cubes and 212 horses for 1954. By 1955, Packard was poised to produce a tremendously impressive Caribbean, since all the firm's plans had finally come to fruition: V-8 engine, Torsion-Level suspension, Twin-Ultramatic Drive, and a gee-whiz facelift courtesy of designer Dick Teague. The two-year problem of having only the junior wheelbase for its upmarket convertible was solved when Packard turned to plastic tooling for a five-inch-longer 127-inch-wheelbase body.

Equipped with Teague's massive egg-crate grille, three-tone paint job, bejeweled dashboard, and cushy leather upholstery, the '55 Caribbean came with Twin-Ultramatic gearbox, Torsion-Level suspension, dual antennas/ exhausts/hood scoops, radio, heater,

Packard marketed the 1955 Caribbean primarily as a flagship model, with the emphasis on unbridled luxury. But that image also required power, and Packard complied with a new 352-cid V-8, dual four-barrel carbs, and 275 horsepower.

and power everything. The only options were wire wheels ($325), tinted ($32) or shaded ($45) glass, and air conditioning. The mighty flagship also boasted the most powerful Packard V-8 engine: 275 horsepower, compliments of dual Rochester carburetors with progressive linkage—four barrels in operation full time, the other four kicking in as required. Only the Chrysler 300 could claim more power.

Of course all of the standard equipment packed into the Caribbean made it heavy—4755 pounds—but with 355 lbs/ft torque at 2400-2800 rpm on tap it could still zip from 0-60 in about 12 seconds and from 50-80 in about 13. And although the '55 Packards weren't seen on race tracks, the firm was proud to point out that between October 22-

It's ironic that Packard produced only 500 '55 Caribbean convertibles (*left*), when in fact more could have been sold. The '56 Caribbean (*opposite, bottom*) kept the three-tone paint, but received detail changes, particularly at the front end. In addition, the engine (*below*) was bored to 374 cubic inches and the compression upped to 10.0:1. Again fed by two Rochester four-barrel carburetors, horsepower took a healthy jump to 310.

1955-56 Packard Caribbean Major Specifications

Engine:	ohv V-8 **1955** 352.0 cid (4.00 × 3.50-in. bore × stroke, 8.5:1 c.r., 2 Rochester 4-bbl carbs, 275 bhp **1956** 374 cid (4.13 × 3.50), 10.0:1 c.r., 2 Rochester 4-bbl carbs, 310 bhp
Transmission:	Twin-Ultramatic automatic
Suspension, front:	independent, longitudinal torsion bars
Suspension, rear:	live axle, longitudinal torsion bars
Brakes:	front/rear drums
Wheelbase (in.):	127.0
Weight (lbs):	4,590-4,960
Top speed (mph):	120
0-60 mph (sec):	11.0-12.0
Base price:	$5,932-$5,995
Production:	**1955** cvt 500 **1956** cvt 276 htp cpe 263

31, 1954, it had achieved "a new milestone in speed" in a '55 Patrician. Under the watchful eye of the American Automobile Association (AAA) Contest Board, the Packard traveled 25,000 miles at an average speed of 104.7 mph, in the process racking up 147 individual records. Among them: 10 World Unlimited records for all distances from 10,000 to 25,000 miles, all daily records from three to seven days, eight International Class B records, 12 U.S. National Unlimited records, 14 U.S. National Class B records, 55 U.S. National Unlimited records for Closed Cars, and 48 U.S. National Class B—Closed Car records. Alas, these records were not accorded international recognition because the enduro was run at Packard's Utica, Michigan, test track—an unrecognized circuit. Unofficial or no, these accomplishments certainly proved the power and durability of Packard's new V-8.

A 1/8-inch bore increase brought the largest Packard engine for 1956 to 374 cid, again the industry's largest. The lightly facelifted Caribbean, now with a hardtop model, returned as the most powerful Packard, with two four-barrel carbs and an unheard of 10.0:1 compression ratio, which resulted in 310 horsepower and 405 lbs/ft torque at 2800 rpm. *Motor Life* clocked the 290-bhp Patrician sedan at 4.0 seconds 0-30, 11.5 seconds 0-60, and 12.5 seconds 50-80. Top speed, meanwhile, settled in at about 120 mph. All in all, *ML* was quite impressed with the various features of the '56 Packard, figuring they "should be a big factor in winning Packard its share of buyers in the luxury car market."

Performance, good looks, a truly innovative suspension system, and luxury brought Packard modest success in 1955, helped in part by the imagemaker Caribbean. Sales nearly doubled 1954 levels, and even Caribbean sales rose from 400 to 500, and could have been higher had Packard not underestimated demand. The company enthusiastically released a mild facelift for 1956, but in fact the 1955 recovery had not been sufficient, nor nearly what Packard needed. Output still remained far below most pre-1954 figures and a spate of service troubles and poor assembly quality in 1955 did further damage in the marketplace. Though 539 Caribbeans were built, sales fell again—the '56 was destined to be the last of the big Packard luxury cars.

1958 Packard Hawk

The most bizarre and interesting 1958 Packard certainly had to be the Hawk, a $4000 supercharged line-leader based on the Studebaker Golden Hawk, with special styling by Duncan McRae. Its front-end design stood apart—unique and completely unforgettable: a wide-mouth grille that looked as if it had been inspired by Electrolux. Other odd features included exterior leather armrests along the side windows, a spare tire outline on the rear deck, and gaudy gold mylar inserts for the flared tailfins. However, McRae did manage to avoid quad headlamps, considered essential for the other '58 Packards. But the car's styling wasn't entirely McRae's responsibility, but without him there probably wouldn't have been a Packard Hawk.

"Mr [Roy] Hurley [Studebaker-Packard chairman] had seen a Ferrari and a Mercedes 300SL during one of his European trips," McRae recalled, "and insisted that a special Hawk be designed to imitate them. The result was what we smilingly called the 'Hurley Hawk'...a perfect example of the wrong idea: overpriced, uncompetitive, overdecorated. Together with the other 1958 Packards it proved a sad end to the marque which expired in mid-year in Studebaker clothing."

Hurley's fascination with the likes of Ferrari and Mercedes explain the Packard's broad scoop grille. Duncan McRae's understanding of the Packard heritage likewise explains the hood indentations or "cusps," which represented the Packard hood shape dating back to 1904. McRae accepted credit for the padded exterior armrests, which reminded him of classic airplanes. The gold mylar tailfins and spare tire impression—likened by stylists to a toilet seat—were simply attempts to set off the Packard Hawk from the Studebaker Hawk, which cost $700 less.

Whatever one thought about the exterior styling, the interior sported beautifully finished pleated leather seats, leather padded dash, and what *Motor Life* described as "the finest instrumentation setup now being used in an American-built car. It's elegantly simple, attractive and highly functional." Set against an engine-turned steel panel were easy-to-read gauges and dials with white markings on black backgrounds. And there were plenty of them: large round speedometer and tachometer, plus fuel, ammeter, oil pressure, water temperature, and manifold pressure gauges.

The last was included because the Packard Hawk ran with Studebaker's 289-cubic-inch supercharged V-8. And with 275 horsepower and 333 lbs/ft torque to motivate a 3470-pound car, it could run. *Motor Life* flashed from 0-30 mph in 3.6 seconds, 0-45 in 6.1, and 0-60 in 9.2. This was with the three-speed Flight-O-Matic slushbox, but *ML* figured that a Hawk with the optional three-speed-plus-overdrive gearbox and 4.09:1 rear axle would knock a half-second off the 0-60 time. With the right gearing, top speed was about 125 mph.

Not only could the Hawk accelerate, it could handle, too. Features included a slightly lower center of gravity, improved steering gear, larger diameter stabilizer bar, and longer rear springs with the axle mounted ahead of their center point. According to *Motor Life*, the changes "have helped make the Packard Hawk a better road car than its predecessors. It's capable of cornering faster, with less body lean and more security. It's still no sports car in the true sense of the phrase, but is much closer to the ideal than 1956 or 1957 Golden Hawks."

The controversial styling of the Packard Hawk has always obscured the fact that it was the fastest production Packard ever built. It was a good second and a fraction faster to 60 mph than any of the big Detroit-built Packard V-8s, and marginally quicker than the 1957 Studebaker-based Packard Clipper four-door sedan and wagon, which though supercharged weighed 100-200 pounds more than the '58 Hawk. In fact, *Motor Life* timed a '57 sedan at 10.5 seconds 0-60 mph; *Motor Trend*'s wagon took 11.0 seconds.

The Packard Hawk remains a curiosity—an outgrowth of last-ditch attempts to preserve the Packard name—as hastily abandoned as it was conceived. Not surprisingly, production was low, just 588 units, and the scarcity of surviving examples has made the Hawks the most collectible of the 1957-58 "Packardbakers." That it was also the fastest car to ever wear the Packard crest is an added bonus!

The 1957-58 Packards have long been derided as "Packardbakers" because they were Studebaker-based and built in Studebaker's South Bend, Indiana, plant. Though looked down upon because of their parentage and because of controversial styling, the supercharged 1958 Packard Hawk was nonetheless an excellent handler and performer. It could romp from 0-60 in nine seconds, give or take a few tenths, and would be doing 125 mph before running out of breath. That made it the fastest Packard of all time—a fact conveniently ignored by enthusiasts of the *true* luxury Packards that were built in Detroit for more than a half century.

1958 Packard Hawk
Major Specifications

Engine:	ohv V-8, 289 cid (3.56 × 3.63-in. bore × stroke), 7.5:1 c.r., 2-bbl carb, supercharger, 275 bhp
Transmission:	3-speed Flight-O-Matic automatic; overdrive opt.
Suspension, front:	variable-rate coil springs, stabilizer bar
Suspension, rear:	live axle, semi-elliptic leaf springs
Brakes:	front/rear drums
Wheelbase (in.):	120.5
Weight (lbs):	3,470
Top speed (mph):	125
0-60 mph (sec):	8.7-9.2
Base price:	$3,995
Production:	588

1956 Plymouth Fury

Part of a quartet of high-performance limited editions from Chrysler, the Plymouth Fury bowed at the Chicago Automobile Show on January 10, 1956. While it used the Savoy/Belvedere hardtop body, it was immediately recognizable via its standard eggshell white finish and full-length bodyside sweepspear of gold anodized aluminum. Gold also decorated the grille center and special "spoke" wheel covers, which bore a resemblance to Cadillac's "Sabre Spokes."

Inside, the Fury sported a special interior in colors to match the vivid exterior: gold leather bolsters with black jacquard inserts. The dashboard looked like a regular '56, except that a tachometer occupied the blank space to the right of the speedometer. All this fancy trim looked very good on the mildly finned '56 body, but what really made the Fury memorable was what happened when you floored the accelerator pedal.

In addressing performance, Fury engineers didn't soup up an existing V-8, like Ford or Chevy. They felt that the standard 277-cid polyspherical-head V-8 needed more displacement for this application, having decided

against chancing any reliability problems with a supercharger. They also avoided a Hemi transplant from other Chrysler divisions, who perhaps weren't cooperative.

What they *did* choose was an engine from across the river: the 303-cubic-inch polyhead from the Canadian Chrysler Windsor/Dodge Royal. This happened to be a good pick because it

fell right at the top of the displacement limit for NASCAR's Class 5 (259-305 cid). To this basic block engineers applied a high-lift cam, solid valve lifters, domed pistons, Carter four-barrel carburetor, free-flow dual exhausts, and 9.25:1-compression heads. The result: 240 horsepower at 4800 rpm, about 0.8 bhp per cubic inch. It's a comment on the pace of the Fifties horsepower race that Chevrolet achieved a full 1.0-bhp per cubic inch just one year later with fuel injection, though the '56 Chrysler 300-B also managed this with high-compression heads.

To handle the extra poke, Furys came equipped with heavy-duty springs and shocks, jumbo Dodge brakes with 11-inch drums, wide 7.10 × 15 tires, and a front anti-sway bar. A heavy-duty three-speed manual transmission with a beefy clutch put the power to the road, though Chrysler's two-speed pushbutton-controlled PowerFlite automatic was optional. The chassis gave the Fury a low, hunkered-down look compared to the taller, high-sided appearance of other Plymouths.

If anybody doubted that the Fury could blow away the cobwebs accumulated from Plymouth's three-decade economy-car role, they had only to read the papers. On the same day the Fury debuted, a pre-production prototype driven by Phil Walters tore up the sands at Daytona Beach, Florida. Fresh from campaigns in his Chrysler-powered Cunningham racing cars, Walters blasted through the flying mile at 124.01 mph, with a best one-way speed of 124.611 mph, and covered the standing mile at 82.54 mph—extraordinary for a near-stock passenger car weighing 3650 pounds.

Just as the Fury was preparing to dominate its class at the Daytona Speed Weeks in February, NASCAR ruled that it hadn't been in production the required 90 days to qualify as "stock." Plymouth replied by running it as a Factory Experimental, using a higher-lift cam, 9.8:1-compression heads, and a Chrysler manifold carrying twin four-barrel carbs. Thus equipped, the Fury scorched through the traps at 143.596 mph—a speed beaten by a Lincoln-engined Mercury, but impressive nonetheless.

Despite a base price of $2866, $550 more than a Belvedere V-8 hardtop, the Fury sold well for a specialty model. It was almost as hot in "street" guise as modified: 0-60 in 9.0-9.6 seconds, the quarter-mile in 16.5 seconds, and top speed of about 115 mph, according to the buff books. The Fury impressed everyone with its combination of speed and agility, even *Road & Track*: "... one of the best handling domestic sedans we have ever driven." Better yet, the '56 Fury was just the first in a long line of high-performance Plymouths.

1956 Plymouth Fury Major Specifications

Engine:	ohv V-8, 303.0 cid (382 × 3.31-in. bore × stroke), 9.25:1 c.r., Carter 4-bbl carb, 240 bhp
Transmission:	3-speed manual; overdrive and 2-speed PowerFlite automatic opt.
Suspension, front:	independent, coil springs, anti-sway bar
Suspension, rear:	live axle, semi-elliptic leaf springs
Brakes:	front/rear drums
Wheelbase (in.):	115.0
Weight (lbs):	3,650
Top speed (mph):	115
0-60 mph (sec):	9.0-9.6
Base price:	$2,866
Production:	4,485

In addition to its 240-bhp V-8 and lowered suspension, the '56 Plymouth Fury sported a unique bodyside spear filled with gold anodized aluminum, gold-trimmed hubcaps from the DeSoto Adventurer (without the "DeS" in the hub), and gold mesh in the center of the grille. One Fury served as an Official Pace Car in Minnesota; another set two U.S. stock car records.

1957-58 Plymouth Fury

Among the fully redesigned 1957 Chrysler Corporation cars, Plymouth perhaps emerged as the most radical, and suggested as much in its ads: "Suddenly It's 1960!" And to enhance the new image, the high-performance Fury boosted its reputation as the most exciting Plymouth. A daringly low beltline, 53 percent more glass on hardtops, fenders level with the hood, and prominent but well-integrated tailfins stood out as the chief design features. The fins were actually aerodynamic, adding directional stability, but only at high speeds.

The '57 Fury again came only as a hardtop, and with the same ivory paint and gold side trim as before. Bowing in mid-December, it was built in limited numbers, but that hardly mattered as Plymouth could barely meet the demand for its regular models. On the new body with its smooth hardtop roofline, Fury hallmarks looked better

than ever. The anodized gold wheel covers of 1956 were dropped, but gold now appeared on the grille bars. Bumper extenders, optional on lesser Plymouths, came standard on the Fury, adding 1.5 inches to overall length. Like its lesser linemates, the '57 Fury rode a three-inch-longer 118-inch wheelbase, and at 53.5 inches high it was an astonishing 5.5 inches lower than the '56. Though wheel diameter shrank an inch, width expanded to six inches, calling for 8.00 × 14 tires.

As in 1956, options included "Full-

Time" power steering, power brakes, air conditioning, electric seat and windows, even dealer-installed seatbelts. Standard Fury goodies encompassed a two-tone steering wheel, variable-speed electric wipers, padded dash and sun visors, foam-rubber seat cushions, and a "sweep-second self-regulating watch."

The '57 Fury came out the chute faster than ever, too, as Chrysler engineers massaged the Canadian 303 V-8 by boring it out to 318 cubic inches. That number would soon become familiar to MoPar enthusiasts, as would the other hot-rodders' tricks employed: dual four-barrel carburetors, high-compression heads, domed pistons, free-flow dual exhausts, high-lift cam, and heavy-duty valve springs. Dubbed the "V-800," this engine delivered 290 horsepower at 5400 rpm and a hefty 325 lbs/ft torque—but at a high 4000 rpm. Incidentally, the V-800 could be

82

The name "Fury" pretty much said it all—Plymouth's 1957 hot rod could really move. It was a looker, too, with gold trim liberally applied over its low, sleek, all-new '57 hardtop body. Heart of the matter was the 318-cubic-inch V-800 engine (*center left*). It employed many hot-rodding tricks: dual four-barrel carbs, high-lift cam, high-compression (9.5:1) heads, domed pistons, and more. The result was 290 horses at 5400 rpm and 325 lbs/ft torque at 4000 rpm. Ads pointed out that this engine was available in any Plymouth and came with a beefed up suspension (*above*).

Hot Rod called the '57 Fury "surely the best handling production car in America." It testers should have known, for the magazine had taken an aerodynamically aided, Chrysler 300-powered '57 Plymouth to the sands of Daytona Beach, Florida (*left*). The '58 Fury (*below, left*) sported a revised grille and taillights, plus an optional 350-cubic-inch Golden Commando V-8 that cranked out 305 horsepower at 5000 rpm and 370 lbs/ft torque at 3600 rpm. Off the line, it could beat the standard V-800 engine to 60 mph by a full second.

tent handling over rough surfaces, and a new level of handling precision. "The Fury will power through hard turns, can be drifted by a true believer," wrote test driver Joe Wherry. *Hot Rod* magazine considered it "surely the best handling production car in America." Perhaps the finest compliment came from *Sports Car Illustrated*: "It's very difficult to adjust to the fact that here is a big Detroit sedan that can easily out-corner many 'bona fide' sports cars."

Like other Plymouths, the '58 Fury carried over the basic '57 package. Again, it sported the distinctive color scheme and gold trim, but quad headlights and "lollipop" taillights were distinguishing features, as were the stock wheel covers with their gold centers.

The V-800 engine remained the same as in 1957, but there was a new option: the "Golden Commando" 350 V-8. Aided by 10.0:1 compression and Carter twin quads, it pumped up 305 horsepower at 5000 rpm. Better yet, its 370 lbs/ft torque came in at a lower 3600 rpm and the torque band was wider, prompting *Road & Track* to say that "the forte of this engine is its tremendous low speed flexibility and torque." Bendix fuel injection was also available, upping output to 315 bhp, but it proved unreliable. It was soon withdrawn, and the few cars so equipped were retro-fitted with twin-quad carbs. In 305-bhp form and with stick shift, 0-60 acceleration now came in at 7.7 seconds according to one contemporary report, just about a second better than the '57 V-800 setup.

Plymouth would continue to use—and abuse—the Fury name into the front-drive age, but it was the hot 1956-58 models that put Plymouth on the performance map.

1957-58 Plymouth Fury Major Specifications

Engine: ohv V-8 **1957-58** 318 cid (3.91 × 3.31-in. bore × stroke), solid valve lifters, 9.5:1 c.r., 2 Carter 4-bbl carbs, 290 bhp **1958** 350 cid (4.06 × 3.38), 10.0:1 c.r., 2 Carter 4-bbl carbs, 305 bhp; Bendix FI, 315 bhp

Transmission: heavy-duty 3-speed manual; 3-speed TorqueFlite automatic opt.

Suspension, front: independent, torsion bars

Suspension, rear: live axle, semi-elliptic leaf springs

Brakes: front/rear drums

Wheelbase (in.): 118.0

Weight (lbs): 3,510-3,595

Top speed (mph): 120-125

0-60 mph (sec): 7.5-9.0

Base price: $2,925-$3,067

Production: **1957** 7,438 **1958** 5,303

ordered for *any* Plymouth, right down to the stripper two-door Plaza—which made the latter quite a Q-ship and inspired many an impromptu drag race. However, even though a high-revving stick-shift Fury could blast through a 0-60-mph run in 8.6 seconds, the smaller Plymouth V-8s with a low-rev torque peak were quicker off the line, though only for a short distance.

Two other developments helped make the '57 Fury memorable. One was Chrysler's new three-speed TorqueFlite automatic transmission, which gained a reputation as America's best automatic, bar none. Still with pushbutton control, it pulled a 3.36:1 rear axle ratio, with other ratios available both for the axle and the standard heavy-duty three-speed manual gearbox.

The second development was torsion-bar front suspension, which put Chrysler Corporation cars at the top of the heap for handling. It provided effortless high-speed cruising, compe-

1956 Pontiac V-8

Most of what's been said for Chevrolet's startling metamorphosis applies to that year's equally altered Pontiac, both of which boasted new V-8 power and a more modern chassis, topped by flashier, more colorful styling.

Chassis improvements centered around a lowered center of gravity, revised front suspension geometry, and rear springs mounted outboard of the side rails. All contributed to better roadholding, if not ride, while larger brakes assured shorter stopping distances.

It's often been true that Pontiac follows where Chevrolet leads, and so it was with 1955 styling. Superstructure, including GM's trendy "Panoramic" wrapped windshield, was dictated by Chevy's all-new A-body, but designer Paul Gillan gave Pontiac its own distinct look below the beltline. The result, riding 120- and 122-inch wheelbases (compared to Chevy's 115), was

generally pleasing, save for the rather unfortunate blunt front. Ever-quotable veteran auto tester Tom McCahill said it made the car look "like it was born on its nose."

Pontiac's biggest '55 bombshell came in the form of a modern overhead-valve V-8. Called Strato-Streak, it featured innovative ball-stud rocker-arm mounts, which were also used on Chevy's new V-8. However, the 287.2-cid Pontiac unit was unique in having the right cylinder bank cast slightly forward of the left to simplify distributor positioning and drive. Other exclusives included efficient "gusher valve" cooling, a harmonic vibration damper, tapered valve guides, fully machined combustion chambers and, per GM practice, hydraulic valve lifters.

The product of some three million development miles, the Strato-Streak delivered 173/180 horsepower standard (stick/Hydra-Matic) with a two-barrel carb and 7.4:1/8.0:1 compression, or 200

For 1956, Pontiac was modestly restyled with a new grille and side trim that reshaped the bodyside two-toning. Also new were three Catalina hardtop sedans. The mid-range 870 Chieftain Catalina two-door hardtop seen here sold for $2840 and output reached 24,744 units.

bhp with a $35 four-barrel-carburetor option. *Motor Trend* tested both the 180- and 200-bhp Strato-Streaks with Hydra-Matic, achieving 0-60 mph in 13.8 and 12.7 seconds, respectively, a marked improvement over the trusty old straight-eight engine.

After record 1955 sales of 553,808 units, Pontiac settled for a modest facelift for 1956. This consisted mainly of a new grille, revised side trim and two-toning, and the addition of three Catalina four-door hardtops to the lineup. Of course, Pontiac had to keep pace in the horsepower race, so it bored out the Strato-Streak to 316.6 cubic inches. With a four-barrel carb and 8.9:1

compression, it cranked out 227 horses at 4800 rpm and 312 lbs/ft torque at 3000 rpm. This engine came standard on the top-line Star Chiefs (optional on Chieftains), mated to the "fluid-flow" Strato-Flight Hydra-Matic gearbox. *Motor Trend*, wringing out this combination in a four-door sedan, did 0-60 mph in 11.4 seconds, the quarter-mile in 18. Stick shift cars got lower 7.9:1 compression and 216 bhp, and were just as fast.

Chieftains made do with a two-barrel carb. With automatic: 8.9:1 compression, 205 bhp at 4600 rpm, and 294 lbs/ft at 2600 rpm. With the three-speed manual: 7.9:1 squeeze, 192 bhp.

Feeling the heat of competition, Pontiac unleashed its hottest Strato-Streak yet in January: 10.0:1 compression, twin four-barrels, special intake manifold and cams, and other beefed-up engine parts. The result was 285 rollicking horses at 5100 rpm. Pontiac said this engine, of which an estimated 200 were produced, was "for those who wish to race professionally or who vie with each other in having a 'hot' performing car." *Motor Trend* laid hands on a Chieftain four-door hardtop with this setup—but walked away disappointed. Around town, the high-lift cam and rough idle were no fun,

and there was no chance for flat-out desert runs because the engine was hardly broken in. *MT* testers noted no significant performance gain over the 227-bhp Star Chief.

But someone else *did*: race driver Ab Jenkins, the spry 73-year-old "King of Speed." On June 26, 1956, under NASCAR supervision, he assaulted the Salt Flats at Bonneville, Utah, in a stock Chieftain two-door sedan. There he set a new 24-hour world endurance record at an average speed of 118.375 miles per hour, *including* 28 pit stops. The fastest 10-mile run was at 126.65 mph, the first 100 miles were clocked at 126.02 mph, and the total distance covered was 2841 miles. Pontiac bragged that only one quart of oil had been added despite temperatures as high as 130 degrees in the sun, and ads soon shouted "Pontiac blazes to new world's record." They also proclaimed that "Pontiac delivered more miles per gallon than any other 'Eight' in *any* class" in the Mobilgas Economy Run.

Production was down industry-wide in 1956, in Pontiac's case to 405,429 units. But no matter—in two short years, Pontiac had laid the groundwork to become a force to be reckoned with in the showroom or on the street. Enthusiasts have been grateful ever since.

1956 Pontiac V-8 Major Specifications	
Engine:	ohv V-8, 316.6 cid (3.94 × 3.25-in. bore × stroke): 2-bbl carb, 7.9:1 c.r., 192 bhp (stick); 8.9:1 c.r., 205 bhp (Hydra-Matic); 4-bbl carb, 7.9:1 c.r., 216 bhp (stick); 8.9:1 c.r., 227 bhp (Hydra-Matic); 10.0:1 c.r., 2 Rochester 4-bbl carbs, 285 bhp
Transmission:	3-speed manual; Dual-Range Hydra-Matic (Chieftains) and Strato-Flight Hydra-Matic (Star Chief) opt.
Suspension, front:	upper and lower A-arms, coil springs
Suspension, rear:	live axle, semi-elliptic leaf springs
Brakes:	front/rear drums
Wheelbase (in.):	**Chieftains** 122.0 **Star Chief** 124.0
Weight (lbs):	3,452-3,797
Top speed (mph):	110-125
0-60 mph (sec):	10.0-13.0
Base price:	$2,240-$3,129
Production:	Chieftain 860 4d sdn 41,987 2d sdn 41,908 Catalina 2d htp 46,335 Catalina 4d htp 35,201 4d wgn 12,702 2d wgn 6,099 Chieftain 870 4d sdn 22,082 Catalina 2d htp 24,744 Catalina 4d htp 25,372 4d wgn 21,674 Star Chief 4d sdn 18,346 cvt 13,510 Custom Catalina 2d htp 43,392 Custom Catalina 4d htp 48,035 Safari 2d wgn 4,042

Opposite page: The rarest of the 1956 Pontiacs was the Custom Safari wagon, a two-door with hardtop-like styling. Officially a Star Chief, it rode a wheelbase two inches shorter than other models in that series. Like them, however, it received top-grade trim and, at $3129, outpriced them all. Maybe that's why only 4042 were built. *This page*: The 870 Chieftain Catalina (*top*) came with a 316.6-cid Strato-Streak V-8 (*center left*), but with 205 bhp as standard, compared to 227 for Star Chiefs. Even on this mid-line Pontiac, the interior (*above*) was nicely done. Second only to the Safari on the price scale was the $2857 Star Chief Deluxe soft top (*left*).

1957 Pontiac Bonneville

Semon E. "Bunkie" Knudsen—fresh from successful managerial stints at GM's Allison and Detroit Diesel divisions—took over the reins at Pontiac in mid-1956. Despite a first-time V-8 and all-new styling in 1955, not to mention a performance push in 1956, Knudsen determined that Pontiac still had to shed its "old man's car" image.

He quickly secured a new chief engineer, future GM president Elliot M. "Pete" Estes, and put him to work on extra carburetors and higher compression. One of the first fruits of his labors appeared during model year '57: the legendary Tri-Power setup, a trio of two-barrel Rochester carbs atop the newly stroked 347-cubic-inch version of Pontiac's versatile 1955 V-8. With 10.0:1 compression and hydraulic lifters, the engines were good for 290 horses with Hydra-Matic, or 317 bhp in NASCAR-certified form with stick shift and dual-breaker ignition, or with Hydra-Matic

and single-breaker ignition. With the 290-bhp unit, 0-60 came up in just 8.5 seconds in a two-door sedan; some other reports placed that figure under eight seconds given ideal conditions.

Next Bunkie hired famed Daytona Beach speed merchant Smokey Yunick to prepare Tri-Power for the track, and a Knudsen-sponsored car ran a record 131.747 mph in the flying mile at that year's Daytona Speed Weeks (officially NASCAR International Performance and Safety Trials by then). Pontiac also won in standing mile acceleration and finished the 160-mile Grand National race at an average 101.6 mph, 11 mph faster than the old record. When the Automobile Manufacturers Association agreed to its anti-racing "edict" in early '57, Knudsen took Pontiac performance underground, retaining Yunick for development work and later resuming ties with tuner Ray Nichels.

Bunkie had something else up his sleeve for '57: a hot limited-edition model to bring throngs of performance-seekers into Pontiac showrooms. It bowed in February with a perfect name: Bonneville, after the Utah Salt Flats where most everybody went to hopefully set speed records. Announced at $5782—when a Star Chief ragtop listed at $3105—and mainly "for

dealer use only," the Bonneville bowed as the costliest and most muscular Pontiac yet. The most luxurious, too. Offered only as a convertible on the top-line Star Chief's 124-inch wheelbase, it came with Strato-Flight Hydra-Matic, and practically everything else on Pontiac's options list. Trim was naturally the best, too, including leather upholstery and deluxe carpeting.

Outside, the Bonneville sported anodized-aluminum gravel shields on the lower rear fenders, hash-mark front-fender trim, chrome-plated bullets set within the spear-like bodyside moldings adopted as part of this year's restyle, and unique spinner wheel covers. The result looked longer and lower than other '57 Pontiacs.

The Bonneville's main technical attraction was advertised on bold front-fender nameplates that read "Fuel-Injection." This referred to a 10.0:1 compression 347 V-8 bored to 370 cubic inches. Though Pontiac never divulged the exact figure, this "fuelie" achieved 310-315 horsepower at 4800 rpm and a mighty 400 lbs/ft torque at 3400 rpm via a new Rochester system similar to the Ramjet option introduced that same year at Chevrolet. But it was a tidier setup allegedly designed for maximum low-range torque rather than top-end

At $5782, some people might have thought the new '57 Pontiac Bonneville convertible (*above and opposite, top*) overpriced. And given that a Star Chief ragtop went for $3105, perhaps they were right. On the other hand, the Bonneville was deliberately built as a limited-edition styling and engineering flagship intended to give the old Chief a more youthful image. The engine in particular (*opposite, bottom*) appealed to young hot bloods because of its 370-cubic-inch size, high 10.0:1 compression ratio, and galloping 310-315 horses. But its main point of interest was that new engineering marvel, fuel injection.

power. It consisted of separate fuel and air meters on a special assembly sitting where the carburetor and intake manifold normally would. Fuel was injected directly into each port, making this what we'd now call a mechanical "multi-port" system.

For all that, the fact is that the Bonneville ragtop outweighed the lightest Chieftain sedans by more than 700 pounds, and the experts said that Tri-Power was slightly more powerful than the fuel-injected V-8. One magazine timed a Bonneville at 18 seconds in the standing quarter-mile—fast but not breathtaking. No matter, because the first Bonneville was mainly a promotional exercise, which is why only 630 were built. But it provided just the sort of sales tonic Pontiac needed, and it worked, in good part because the Bonneville was in fact a "muscle car" in its time.

"You can sell an old man a young man's car," Bunkie once said, "but you can never sell a young man an old man's car." With the '57 Bonneville, Pontiac wouldn't do that again for a long, long time. Perhaps that's why the Bonneville is still with us, and in addition to a much more sophisticated electronic fuel injection system, it's also supercharged!

1957 Pontiac Bonneville Major Specifications

Engine:	ohv V-8, 370 cid (4.06 × 3.56-in. bore × stroke), 10.0:1 c.r., Rochester FI, 310-315 bhp est.
Transmission:	4-speed Strato-Flight Hydra-Matic automatic
Suspension, front:	upper and lower A-arms, coil springs
Suspension, rear:	live axle, semi-elliptic leaf springs
Brakes:	front/rear drums
Wheelbase (in.):	124.0
Weight (lbs):	4,285
Top speed (mph):	125
0-60 mph (sec):	8.1
Base price:	$5,782
Production:	630

Setting the Bonneville apart from everyday Pontiacs were anodized-aluminum gravel shields on the lower rear fenders, hash-mark front-fender trim, chrome-plated bullets set within the spear-like bodyside moldings adopted as part of the 1957 restyle, and unique spinner wheel covers. And, of course, "FUEL INJECTION" was emblazoned in large letters on the front fenders. Even the name set this special Pontiac apart—the Bonneville was named after the famed Utah Salt Flats where hopeful drivers went to set speed records.

1957 Rambler Rebel

What a wonderful contradiction: a Rambler Rebel. How could that be? Wasn't Rambler that little Nash, the one that had become almost synonymous with affordable, no-nonsense transportation since 1950? Sure. *Everybody* knew what a Rambler was: slow but thrifty, small but comfortable, reliable and—well—dull. Yet suddenly, American Motors sprung on an unsuspecting public a Rebel: a flashy silver four-door hardtop with gold bodyside sweepspears, "continental" spare tire—and a bigger V-8 than anything found at Chevrolet, Ford, or Plymouth. So this was hardly a Rambler—it could embarrass most any car at any stoplight in America.

Some might say that this strange turn of events came as a subtle sign that AMC, formed via a merger of Nash and Hudson on May 1, 1954, would soon give up on the Nashes and Hudsons—at least in name—and put all its chips on the Rambler. As only 1500 samples were built, the '57 Rebel was obviously never intended to make money, especially at its $2786 base

price. But it did introduce the public to a new name—and the idea that at least some future Ramblers might not be economy compacts.

The car itself was straightforward enough. Its big attraction lurked under the hood: a new AMC-designed 327-cubic-inch V-8, engineered by David Potter and first seen a bit earlier on the full-size Nashes and Hudsons. With a four-barrel carburetor and dual exhausts, it developed a healthy 255 horsepower. It was as modern a V-8 as most anything from the Big Three: five-main-bearing crankshaft, cast-iron head, aluminum-alloy pistons with three steel-insert rings. These features, as well as the basic block and a short 3.25-inch stroke were shared with the smaller 250-cid V-8 offered optionally for the first time in lesser '57 Ramblers. A half-inch-larger 4.00-inch bore accounted for the increased displacement.

This big engine made the mid-size Rebel one of 1957's hottest performers. No wonder—this was the same formula Pontiac would use with its 1964

If ever there was a sleeper in the '50s, it was the Rambler Rebel. Everyone knew that Ramblers were small and thrifty—and slow. How then, a *rebellious* Rambler, one that could beat just about any 1957 car from 0-60, except perhaps a Corvette?

hot rod, the GTO. In the Rebel, this resulted in a power-to-weight ratio of about 13 lbs/bhp, which looked good even in the muscle-car Sixties. To handle it, AMC fitted Gabriel adjustable shocks and heavy-duty springs all-around, plus an anti-roll bar at each end. Power steering came standard, as did the power brakes that all Rambler Customs received. Bendix electronic fuel injection had been planned, which would have increased output to about 288 horses, but due to development problems it never materialized.

Not that it was really needed. AMC sent a Rebel down for press evaluation to the sands of Daytona Beach, Florida, where *Motor Trend* auto tester Joe Wherry recorded an average of just 7.5 seconds for the benchmark 0-60-mph

The Rebel stood out from other Ramblers via silver paint set off with unique gold sweepspears and a "continental" spare tire (*top and bottom*)—and specific badging (*center left*). What made it hot was a 255-bhp 327 V-8 (*center right*) that hurled the Rebel from 0-60 in 7.5 seconds. An intermediate with AMC's biggest V-8, the Rebel was arguably the first "muscle car," beating out Pontiac's legendary GTO by seven years!

sprint. "From a steady 50 mph in overdrive," he wrote, "the needle hits a corrected 80, with sudden kickdown slapping the box back into third, in just 7.2 seconds. This is high performance, believe me, when family cars are under discussion." Or any other kind of car, for that matter, even decades later.

Wherry judged Rebel handling "fine—not superb, but improved over the regular Rambler line... [the suspension upgrades] minimize roll, make nose-diving on fast stops very slight indeed, and prevent bottoming except...where speed is extreme. The torque-tube driveline prevents rear-axle wind-up on fast takeoffs. [Road feel] is good even with power steering...although the lock is too great (nearly four turns)." Wherry reported some brake fade in repeated high-speed applications, but said "the Rebel sho-'nuff ain't the only power-packed critter with brakes that need beefing up...."

The ultimate compliment, however, was that *Motor Trend* figured that the only production car capable of out-accelerating a '57 Rebel from 0-60 miles per hour was a fuel injected Corvette. How's that for ramblin' along?

1957 Rambler Rebel Major Specifications

Engine:	ohv V-8, 327 cid (4.00 × 3.25-in. bore × stroke), 9.5:1 c.r., Carter 4-bbl carb, 255 bhp
Transmission:	3-speed manual; overdrive or GM 4-speed Dual-Range Hydra-Matic opt.
Suspension, front:	upper and lower A-arms, coil springs, anti-roll bar
Suspension, rear:	live axle, coil springs, anti-roll bar
Brakes:	front/rear drums
Wheelbase (in.):	108.0
Weight (lbs):	3,353
Top speed (mph):	115+
0-60 mph (sec):	7.5
Base price:	$2,786
Production:	1,500

1956-57 Studebaker Golden Hawk

Evolving from the 1955 Speedster concept—a four/five-seater coupe featuring European-style sports-car characteristics—Studebaker's Hawks arguably preceded the Ford Mustang by eight years as the original "pony-car." Be that as it may, the Hawks have never been recognized for this because they had far less influence on the marketplace. Still, the Hawk is significant historically, and a fine car in its own right, logically taking the '53 "Loewy" Starliner coupe a step further in its evolution—and packing performance that the original could only hint at.

In 1956, its initial year, Studebaker built the Hawk in four flavors. The pillared six-cylinder Flight and 259 V-8 Power Hawks winged it beneath the 289 Sky Hawk hardtop. Flying above them all was the Golden Hawk, a pillarless coupe that soared with the help of a big Packard V-8 with optional Ultramatic Drive. With its distinctive classic, square grille, stubby fiberglass tailfins, and luxurious interior in vinyl or vinyl-and-cloth, it naturally attracted the

most attention with auto buffs. Definitely in the hot car class, it competed with two-seaters like the Thunderbird.

Unfortunately, the Golden Hawk had one major drawback—it had a droopy beak. The Packard engine weighed a good 100 pounds more than the Studebaker 289, itself no lightweight, causing the car to understeer with single-minded consistency, sometimes even interfering with acceleration. "Due to the tremendous torque of the engine (380 lbs/ft at 2800 rpm) *and* due to the [heavy engine], it is almost impossible to make a fast getaway start on any surface without considerable wheel spinning," wrote the veteran road tester Tom McCahill of *Mechanix Illustrated*. "If I'd shoved 200 or 300 pounds of sand in the trunk to equalize the weight distribution, my times would have been considerably better."

True, perhaps, but the Golden Hawk was one of the few cars on the 1957 market that, without an optional "Power Pack" or special dealer-installed hop-up goodies, could acceler-

The '56 Studebaker Golden Hawk (*top*) ran with Packard's 352-cid V-8 tuned to 275 horsepower. The result was advertised as the "most power-per-pound of any American car" (*above*), which meant 0-60 in 8.7 seconds and 60-100 mph in 17.7 seconds.

ate from 0-60 mph in less than 10 seconds. In fact, contemporary test reports averaged just over nine seconds with Ultramatic, just under with stick shift/overdrive.

Facelifted afresh, the '57 Golden Hawk tried to keep pace with styling trends by adding tall, steel, concave fins to replace the little fiberglass units of 1956. And without altering the classic square-mesh radiator grille and ribbed rear deck, the bright trim was cleaned up to complement the two-toning that was now restricted to those tailfins. Fortunately, the fully instrumented and purposeful instrument panel was carried over.

Under the skin, many differences quickly became apparent. First off, the Studebaker 289 V-8 replaced the Packard unit, and variable-rate front coil springs and optional Twin-Traction limited-slip differential—which provided up to 80 percent of engine power to the rear wheel with the best

grip—were new, and so was a luxury leather-outfitted "400" model. But easily the most interesting feature of the '57 Golden Hawk was its McCulloch centrifugal supercharger, which was driven by a belt taken off the crankshaft pulley through a planetary ball mechanism, which increased impeller speed 4.4 times over belt speed. The impeller was activated by a solenoid built into the accelerator linkage; its speed was variable—controlled by the position of the pedal. At medium cruise, the blower freewheeled, delivering only about 1.5 pounds per square inch of boost. Depressing the accelerator increased boost pressure to 5.0 psi. On the 289, the blower boosted horsepower by 22 percent, which meant that the smaller Studebaker V-8 cranked out the same 275 bhp as the big Packard V-8. Though the supercharged Hawk was down nearly 50 lbs/ft of torque (333 lbs/ft), this was offset by the lighter engine.

Other than McCahill, few testers had condemned the nose-heavy characteristics of the '56 Golden Hawk, but in 1957, when the lighter Stude V-8 took over, they outdid each other by noting what an improvement it was. And indeed it was, for acceleration times hadn't changed a whit—0-60 still around nine seconds and the quarter-mile at 17.3 seconds—but handling was sharper. *Hot Rod* magazine said that the '57 was "as far removed from its '56 namesake as it is from a Sherman tank. [It] can cut a pretty fancy corner without any of the front end 'wash out' displayed by the '56." It's too bad that only 4071 and 4356 individualistic souls in 1956-57 (and only 878 in 1958) had the nerve to buck the "don't buy an orphan" fear of most buyers. Perhaps the majority that steered away from the Studebaker dealerships were right; likely they wouldn't have understood the pleasures of motoring in a Golden Hawk anyway.

1956-57 Studebaker Golden Hawk Major Specifications	
Engine:	ohv V-8 **1956** 352 cid (4.00 × 3.50-in. bore × stroke), 9.5:1 c.r., 4-bbl carb, 275 bhp **1957** 289 cid (3.56 × 3.63), 7.8:1 c.r., 2-bbl carb, supercharger, 275 bhp
Transmission:	**1956** overdrive; Ultramatic automatic opt. **1957** 3-speed manual; overdrive or 3-speed Flight-O-Matic automatic opt.
Suspension, front:	independent, coil springs, tube shocks
Suspension, rear:	live axle, semi-elliptic leaf springs, tube shocks
Brakes:	front/rear finned drums
Wheelbase (in.):	120.5
Weight (lbs):	**1956** 3,360 **1957** 3,185
Top speed (mph):	120-125
0-60 mph (sec):	8.5-9.5
Base price:	$3,061-$3,182
Production:	**1956** 4,071 **1957** 4,356

The '57 Studebaker Golden Hawk (*both pages*) received a "taillift" comprising taller fins and cleaner side trim. Two-toning, restricted to the fins, was also neater. However, when Studebaker-Packard was forced by economic necessity to shut down Packard's Detroit plants, the Hawk lost its big V-8. Since there wasn't room to enlarge Stude's 289 V-8, the solution hit upon was to bolt on a McCulloch supercharger. The result was the same 275 horsepower as in 1956, but about 50 lbs/ft less torque. In the end, this didn't matter because the lighter 289 V-8 not only saved weight, it improved weight distribution. Performance remained about the same—Studebaker's claimed 8.7 seconds 0-60—but the handling was far better.

INDEX